Ellen White:
Trailblazer
for God

Other books by Paul B. Ricchiuti

Ellen White: Friend of Angels

Books for Children
Camp Meeting Angel/The Little Girl Who Giggled

Charlie Horse/Mrs. White's Secret Sock

Mr. Squirrel's Treasure/Ellen's Miracle Horse

Where's Moo Cow?/Tig's Tale

Uncle Paul's Little Learning Books,
My Very Best Friend: A Lesson About Jesus

Uncle Paul's Little Learning Books,
Let's Play Make-Believe: A Lesson About Heaven

Uncle Paul's Little Learning Books,
Elijah Jeremiah Phillips's Great Journey: A Lesson About God's Care

Uncle Paul's Little Learning Books,
Five Little Gifts: A Lesson About God's Love

Ellen White:
Trailblazer for God

More stories from her amazing adventures, travels, and relationships

Paul B. Ricchiuti

Pacific Press® Publishing Association
Nampa, Idaho
Oshawa, Ontario, Canada
www.pacificpress.com

Cover design by Dennis Ferree
Cover illustration by Marcus Mashburn

Additional copies of this book are available by calling toll free
1-800-765-6955 or visiting http://www.adventistbookcenter.com

Library of Congress Cataloging-in-Publication data:
Ricchiuti, Paul B.
Ellen White: Trailblazer for God: More stories from her amazing adventures, travels, and relationships/Paul B. Ricchiuti.
p. cm.
Includes bibliographical references.
ISBN: 0-8163-1913-8
1. White, Ellen Gould Harmon, 1827-1915. 2. Seventh-day Adventists—
United States—Biography. I. Title

BX6193.W5 R524 2003
286.7'092—dc21

[B]   2002030350

03 04 05 06 07 • 5 4 3 2 1

Dedication

To the memory of Chuck Knorr,
a great athlete and a wonderful, loyal friend who loved God.
I will look for him when Jesus comes.
I know he will be there.

Acknowledgments

Few books are complete unless they include a number of people or institutions to thank for making them possible. The Ellen G. White Estate is at the top of the list. They always had the right answers when I needed them. Pauline Maxwell, from the White Estate branch office at Andrews University, is a real jewel. She not only is helpful but is a model of politeness itself. She and William Fagal, also from the White Estate, are two people I could not have written this book without.

And how can I ever thank friends who encouraged me to keep going when things failed? A few are Tim Larson, Ron and Jim Wilmot, Peggy Pottle, Naomi and Jim Babb, Cheryl Snyder, Deanna Davis, Bonnie Tyson-Flyn, and Frances Scott.

Last, I can never thank Ed Quiring enough for correcting and editing this manuscript. He would not like to be listed last in the acknowledgments. However, to him I will just say this: Remember, Ed, the first shall be last, and the last shall be first.

Thank you again to each and every one of you.

Paul B. Ricchiuti
Nampa, Idaho

Contents

Preface

Before you start reading, I would like to tell a story. It is about the young man in my dedication. As you may have read, his name was Chuck Knorr.

A number of years ago, I was the youth leader for the Mountain View Seventh-day Adventist Church in California. One of my assignments was to become acquainted with all new young people who came to the church. In this way, I could introduce them to the other youth of the church.

One Sabbath a young couple was introduced to me. I was more than impressed by what I saw. The young man was extremely handsome, and from his appearance he had to be an athlete. The girl was an exceptionally beautiful blonde. Both had come to the Mountain View area because of the Santa Clara Swim Club. They were both expert divers. The center in Santa Clara is for advanced swimmers and divers, specializing in training candidates for the Olympics.

The young man's name was Chuck Knorr, and at that time he held the title of National Youth Diving Championship for the United

States. I later learned that he held the title for three years. He was at the top of his field, a tremendous athlete.

The young woman whose name I cannot recall was also a champion in her field. They made a striking couple. Hollywood could never have done better. They were exceptional.

As time went on, I became close friends with Chuck. We went many places together and were real friends. I remember running with him along the California beaches. I had a hard time just to keep going. It was no problem for him. So, as I huffed and puffed, he was turning flips beside me and laughing. He had endless energy and loved it.

Both Chuck and his friend began taking Bible studies at the church from a woman named Mary Walsh. Chuck held back, but the young lady did not. She accepted what she heard and was baptized. This meant giving up her swimming career. She did. She often came to visit me at my office at Pacific Press in Mountain View. She was delightful and a real Christian. I remember introducing her to a friend of mine, whom she later married.

But Chuck went on with his diving career; he had his heart set on competing in the Olympics. I heard later that he did have a chance to try out for the Olympic team. But on the day of the trials, he became nervous and failed by the smallest margin. He was good enough, but it just didn't happen.

Although I didn't see Chuck any longer, I did try to keep track of him. I learned that after failing to make the Olympic team, Chuck felt the Lord did not want him to continue his diving career. So he gave it up and joined the Seventh-day Adventist Church. Next, he went to Andrews University to study.

I made a business trip to Andrews University. And while walking in the administration building with Professor Robert Moon, I asked him about Chuck. "Oh yes," replied my friend. "He is a student here, and he visits local churches, telling his story." Then I was in for a shock, because Professor Moon continued, "And he mentions you."

I caught my breath after that statement and said, "I wish I could see him, but there is no time for that."

Suddenly my friend stopped walking and said as he pointed, "There he is now."

My mouth dropped open and I shouted, "Chuck!"

A young man stopped, turned, and looked in my direction. The hallway was dark, so we couldn't see each other very well. But he started in my direction. And when he stood in front of me, I said, "Chuck, I am Paul Ricchiuti."

There was another shout, books and papers fell to the floor, and Chuck was hugging me so tight I thought I would never be able to breathe again.

He backed off, looked straight at me, and said, "I tell everyone about you." A few words were spoken, the bell rang, and he said, "I have to go to class." As he picked up his books and papers, I told him I had to leave right away too. That was the last time I ever saw Chuck.

A couple of years later, I was in Detroit, Michigan, and needed to contact one of the Adventist churches. When I told the man who answered the phone my name, he said, "Oh, you're Chuck's friend."

I was puzzled. "Chuck who?" I asked.

"Chuck Knorr," came the reply. "I am his stepfather."

I was shocked. "Wow!" I shouted. "Tell me about him. Where is he, and what is he doing?"

In a quiet, calm voice Chuck's stepfather began to tell me. "Chuck," he said, "left Andrews, got married, and the two of them went to Mexico to study medicine. They wanted to become doctors." He continued, "You know what a good athlete Chuck was?"

I answered "Yes," not catching the significance of the word *was*.

"Well," Chuck's stepfather went on. "Both he and his wife were athletic and took up mountain climbing." There was a pause in the conversation. He hesitated then said, "While Chuck was climbing, he lost his hold and fell to his death."

I couldn't talk. His stepfather understood as I stammered something. We hung up. I was crying, and he knew it.

There is a strange twist to this story. In telling my mother about Chuck one day, she shocked me. "I know his mother," she said. I didn't believe it. She went on to tell me that both she and Chuck's mother had attended the old Detroit Grand River Church together. They were friends. Was it possible that when I was a teen, Chuck was one of the little boys running around the church? I had met him clear across the United States, and he had been in my own, so to say, backyard all the time. God works in unusual ways to perform His wonders. His love and care was with Chuck all the time, although he may have not been aware of it for part of his life.

God's guidance is always available if we want it—and I believe Chuck did. God was leading him every step of the way, just as He is doing for every one of us.

Ellen White's life is evidence of God's leading, too, as we shall see.

There is a better place to live than the earth we know. And Jesus has gone ahead of us to make things ready there for our arrival. Life on this planet is not all there is. And if faithful, you, who read this, along with Chuck and me, will go home to be with Jesus forever. Never, never forget that.

Introduction

Writing this book has been one of the most frustrating things I have ever done. It has presented me with one disaster after another. The morning I finished writing the final chapter of this book and was adding the references, my computer screen went blank. Everything was gone, and nothing I could do would bring it back. In desperation, I phoned Robin Russell, who works in the computer department at Pacific Press, and told him what had happened. He came right over. And try as he might, he found nothing. My hard work of about half a year had vanished. Later in the day I contacted Steve Ertel, another computer professional. He listened to Robin and me explain what had happened. And he, too, said there was nothing anyone could do. My entire manuscript was gone.

And so I began to rewrite the manuscript based on my notes and some computer printouts. In time, the manuscript was complete again. I printed out the entire manuscript and laid it aside. If something should happen again to my computer files, I would have a printed copy of the entire manuscript.

When I began to revise my manuscript, all the files vanished again. Robin and Steve again tried to help. My manuscript files had disappeared the second time, and there was no way for any of us to get it back. So, I had to retype the manuscript, using the printed copy.

This was not the first time my writing seemed sabotaged when I attempted to write about Ellen White. Years ago, when I lived in California, I began writing my first book about Ellen White. It took me five years to complete it. Every time I sat down to write, I became ill. It happened over and over again. And when I stopped writing, I felt better. But when I began to research and write, I was sick again. Yet, I never gave up. And slowly, very slowly, the book *Ellen* took shape until it was finally finished.

I had no trouble writing *Ellen White: Friend of Angels,* my second book about Ellen White. And I wondered why. The reason, I now believe, is that the book is pleasant to read and contains little conflict.

We have read how biblical prophets were mistreated. It is no different today. When it comes to the subject of Ellen White, members of the Seventh-day Adventist Church seem to fall into two classes. One group accepts her as a prophet. But unfortunately, sometimes this group misuses her writings by using them as a club, by emphasizing only selected portions, or by elevating them above the Bible. Another group accepts her as a prophet but ignores her writings, claiming that her messages were relevant in her time but no longer in ours. This group neglects to look for the concepts and principles behind what she had to say. Ellen White knew that people would look for excuses to ignore her writings, but it never stopped her work.

Satan's purpose in leading people to either misuse or ignore Ellen White's messages is to keep them from reading God's warning and encouragement to fallen humanity at the end of time. These warnings would reveal Satan's plans and defeat his purpose to destroy every one of us.

I challenge you to read Ellen White's works. And if you do, you will be surprised, challenged, and encouraged by what God has to tell you through one of His faithful and diligent messengers.

CHAPTER ONE

1881

Have you ever had a night when you couldn't sleep? You close your eyes. You picture sheep and start counting. That doesn't work. You open your eyes again. Night sounds float through a window. Leaves brush against each other. In the distance you hear a car door slam. People laugh. A dog barks. And from high overhead comes the sound of a jet. You toss. You turn. You fluff your pillows. You close your eyes. But you just cannot go to sleep.

Then as you lie there, waves of memory bring regrets, smiles—and all the things you must do the next day. Faces, places, forgotten words—they're all there. This happens to every one of us. Ellen White was no exception, especially in her early life, except for the sound of a jet, of course.

In my previous book *Ellen,* I wrote a brief section on the events surrounding the death of James White. Now, I will reveal more detail. And as I do, you may recall a similar time in your life.

Ellen suffered deeply when James died. And the sorrow she felt proved beyond doubt that she was no super-human being. She was like all the rest of us, even enduring sleepless nights. She was just another member of the human race. One thing, however, does set her apart from most people: the vicelike grip she had on her Friend Jesus. That, and that alone, enabled her to survive.

During the first few nights of August 1881, Ellen repeatedly suffered through long, restless, sleepless hours. It was dreadful. Early that month found her desperately ill in Battle Creek Sanitarium. Consciousness came and went, and she was on the verge of becoming delirious. Those were tense moments for the people who attended her. They were either in tears or just shook their heads, sure she was going to die. It was only a matter of time.

She and her husband, James, had been the center of a strange drama a few days earlier. It was sad to watch as strong men carried the Whites from their house to the street, where a hack waited. The carriers tried not to jolt or tilt their heavy load as they steadied James and Ellen on a large mattress covered with blankets. The two were so sick that they needed professional medical care. It was even difficult for either of them to move. They were tenderly placed, mattress and all, into the hack. Then the hack slowly carried James and Ellen through the streets of Battle Creek to the hospital.

There were no ambulances in those days. And an ordinary carriage was out of the question because of its rolling motion. The hack was a better choice. A hack was an early form of taxicab that was pulled by a horse. Its swaying movements could be controlled. Also, those who walked beside it could steady it more easily.

So, as the two lay on the mattress, they were slowly taken to Battle Creek Sanitarium for treatment. Yet even in her weakened condition, Ellen's thoughts were not about herself. They were on James. She was afraid he would not get well.

James and Ellen were placed in separate rooms and cared for by tender, loving attendants. Nurses and doctors—especially Doctor John Harvey Kellogg—worked desperately, with all the knowledge at their command. And slowly, very slowly, Ellen began to respond to their skilled care. But with James it was a different story.

No matter what they did for him, it became increasingly obvious that James was not going to recover. This created a dilemma: Ellen had to be told about her husband. Yet, Dr. Kellogg hesitated to tell her because of her weakened condition. Ellen could have a relapse and slip away along with James. The medical staff knew they had to take that risk and let her know.

Doctor Kellogg broke the news as gently as he could. He also urged Ellen to go to James right away if she wanted to see her husband alive. She insisted on being taken to his room at once. This was a typical Ellen White reaction. She seemed to be at her best in a crisis.

Ellen was carefully carried to James's room. Others were there when she arrived. Uriah Smith and the Whites' son, James Edson, were among them. Willie, their other son, was far away in California.

Ellen took one look at James and knew he was going to die. She asked to be carried as close to him as possible. When this was done, she leaned next to his face and in a quiet tone asked, "Do you want to live?"

No one spoke as husband and wife studied each other. She reached an unsteady hand to touch his forehead and wait for his answer. James's voice was so weak and strained that it was barely audible. His answer was, "No."[1] Now they were both crying. Yet, even through their tears, she and James continued to speak. But it was only what a husband and wife could say to each other.

Just a few weeks before, Ellen had urged James to give up some of the work he was doing. She knew he was badly overworked, and his health was failing. "In reply he spoke of various matters which required attention . . . duties which some one must do. Then with deep feelings he inquired: 'Where are the men to do this work? Where are those who have an unselfish interest in our institutions, and who will stand for the right, unaffected by any influence with which they may come in contact?'

"With tears he expresses his anxiety for our institutions. . . . Said he: 'My life has been given to the upbuilding of these institutions. It seems like death to leave them. They are as my children, and I cannot separate my interest from them. . . . I would rather die than live to see these institutions mismanaged, or turned aside from the purpose for which they were brought into existence.' "[2]

James was now telling Ellen that he had had enough. He had been overworked for years, doing the work of several men, and now the stress of it all had caught up with him.

Now, in a hospital room with Ellen beside him, James was dying.

"Rest," she whispered.

Placing her hand in his, Ellen felt James's fingers tighten around hers. He closed his eyes, and the deep lines that had marked his face began to fade. "Relax," Ellen whispered. His hand tightened again. Then James let go. She slipped her hand away, and the two spoke no more.

James White had given up. He was tired in mind and body and could not go on. He died on August 6, 1881.

James had come a long way. As a child, he was weak, nervous, and cross-eyed. Though he tried to learn to read at an early age, even when a teenager, James could still barely stumble through a simple Bible verse. But at the age of sixteen, James began to gain in strength, and his eyes became normal. And at eighteen he was taller and healthier than most of his friends.

Now, at his death, 2,500 people attended his funeral. He had risen to become one of the best-known religious leaders in the nation. Newspapers throughout the country praised him. George Willard, a former member of Congress said this about him: "As with all true founders of communities, his life is not a broken shaft, but an enduring column, whereon others are to build."[3]

James White had actually worked himself to death, and Ellen was now a widow.

Why did James White's work affect his health? And what kind of stress was he under? "Between 1863 and 1865 the Civil War had been raging. Elder White had 'been heavily taxed in labors in behalf of his brethren who were being drafted into the army.' Always the leader of the church, he felt responsible for everything that happened. Besides, he and his wife were often traveling, usually unable to find proper food or even to get sufficient rest."

With James's workload on her mind, Ellen had this to say: "I was shown that Sabbathkeepers as a people labor too hard without allowing themselves change or periods of rest."[4] This was especially true of the early pioneers in the Seventh-day Adventist Church. They all seemed to travel continually. And many of them, like James White, took on too many jobs and became overworked and tired.

James's health broke down in 1865, following a stroke. Doctors ordered complete bed rest. Ellen did not agree. Instead, she devised several ways to get him active and moving again. She also wanted to get his mind off what he had been doing, which had brought on his sickness. Here is one example of what she did. "Still realizing that James needed outdoor exercise, Ellen White used interesting methods of helping him. Willie wrote, 'Early in May [1866] a piece of land was plowed for us, and then Mother sent to town for three hoes. . . . [He] joined in the planting of corn and beans. During the days that followed, Father and Mother be-stirred [busied] themselves to get berries and trees planted.' "

Willie continues. " 'One day as we were passing close to where large pine trees had recently been cut and taken to a near-by saw-mill, Mother noticed a lot of large pine chips. "Willie, stop," she said. "See those big pine chips. They will be good for the cook stove." Then she climbed out of the carryall (horse-drawn buggy) and began to gather up the chips. "Come James," she called. "Help me pick up these chips." Regretfully he climbed down and helped to gather the chips. When the task was completed, he was glad that he had helped. To Mother the two bushels of chips were worth a few cents, but the victory that Father had gained over inertia was worth to her more than many dollars.' "[5]

Today the methods she used are called "rehabilitation" and "physical therapy." She was ahead of her time.

Fresh air, sunshine, and physical activity all helped James to recover his health. "Before long, James White was strong and able to travel, preach and work so hard that his wife had to warn him against overwork again!"[6]

Did he listen? No. And he suffered fatal consequences be-cause he wouldn't take sound advice.

Ellen White herself came close to dying following James's death. She was still very sick when she went back to her room after he died. But she had insisted on staying with James all night and into the next day until it was over. By then Ellen was near collapse. Doctor Kellogg knew what danger she was in and in-structed two women to stay with her constantly while he napped nearby. His orders were to "watch the pulse and call me at any change."

Ellen did not realize the extent of her danger and felt sorry for the women and even suggested that they go and get some rest.

They stayed with her anyway.

Her pulse stopped at midnight, and Dr. Kellogg was at her side in an instant. By then Ellen was not able to talk and assumed she was going to die. Dr. Kellogg and the two women worked over her until three in the morning. Electric shock was employed as well as applications of ice and heat over her spine. As a result, her pulse slowly grew stronger, although it was weak and fluttery. The battle against death went on for four days. But Ellen White did recover.[7]

Ellen's illness happening at the same time of James's death was one of the most stressful times in Ellen White's life. It shows us that her suffering was as deep as any you or I have ever experienced. After all, this woman was just another human being. Yet, she was a human being with a very special gift from God Himself.

1. Ellen G. White, *Life Sketches of Ellen G. White* (Nampa, Idaho: Pacific Press Publishing Association, 1943), 251.

2. Ibid., 248.

3. Arthur L. White, *Ellen G. White: The Lonely Years, 1876-1891* (Hagerstown, Md.: Review and Herald Publishing Association, 1984), 177.

4. Ellen G. White Estate, "Spirit of Prophecy Emphasis Week for Seventh-day Adventist Schools, 1974," 23.

5. Ibid., 26.

6. Ibid., 27.

7. *The Lonely Years,* 179, 180.

CHAPTER TWO

The Christian's Summer

In chapter one we learned about the time when Ellen maneuvered James into helping her and Willie to pick up wood chips. We also read how he benefited from doing so. But that wasn't the only time Ellen advised people to do activities that we would now call physical therapy. Where did she learn about rehabilitation? Let's find out.

Ellen and James had lost two of their sons in death. Now Willie was sick, and they feared he would be the third. The thought of three graves in the Battle Creek Cemetery overwhelmed them. *Not three,* they thought, *not Willie too.*

John had been the first. Then Henry, who had died of pneumonia. Now Willie had the same illness. We have Willie's own description as to what happened. He is writing in the third person.

"Only a few months before, Mrs. White had been shown in vision that poisonous drugs should not be given and that water treatments would help the sick get well. Now Elder and Mrs. White decided to use simple water treatments rather than drugs."[1]

We will stop here for a moment to explain what Willie meant by "drugs" for treating the sick. Doctors in the nineteenth century used powerful chemicals freely in treating their patients. Among the drugs used were such things as morphine, opium, quinine, and strychnine, along with stimulants, such as tea and coffee, and depressants, such as wine, beer, rum, and brandy.

Now, let's return to our story. Willie is still doing the reporting.

"They placed cold compresses on Willie's head and chest, keeping his feet and hands warm. For five days they prayed and worked untiringly. During this time Willie ate only one small cracker.

"By this time the Mother was exhausted. She went to her room to try to rest. But sleep refused to come—she could only toss restlessly. At last, feeling the need of fresh air, she opened the door to her room into the hall. Soon she was asleep. In a dream she saw an experienced physician standing by the sick child, watching his breathing and feeling his pulse. Turning to Mrs. White he said, 'The crisis has passed. He has seen his worst night. He will recover speedily.' Then the physician continued: 'That which gave you relief will also relieve your child. He needs air. You have kept him too warm. . . . Light and air are excluded from the sick room at the very time when most needed, as though dangerous enemies.' About noon the following day Willie's fever broke and he made a quick recovery."[2]

From that time on, Ellen White was a convert to the beneficial effects of breathing fresh air. When attending camp meetings, Mrs. White was able to combine two things she truly enjoyed—living an outdoor life and speaking to others from the Word of God. She used her camp-meeting experiences to emphasize the benefits of fresh air. "At camp-meetings we have tented out for weeks in succession, sleeping with the ends of the tent open to the air, and we have not suffered with colds," she reported.[3]

I would like to insert something that shows Ellen's love for being out in nature and her eagerness to observe and learn nature's lessons.

When urging parents to use plants and animals to teach children practical lessons, Ellen used birds as one illustration. "Birds," she said, "are teachers of the sweet lesson of trust. Our Heavenly Father provides for them; but they must gather the food, they must build their nests and rear their young. Every moment they are exposed to enemies that seek to destroy them. Yet how cheerily they go about their work! How full of joy are their little songs." [4]

On another occasion, Ellen used unexpected weather to illustrate the Christian life. At a camp meeting in Kansas that was held in October 1878, snow came early. And even though it was cold, no one went home. "Faithful preparation had been made for cold weather," wrote Ellen. "Every tent had a stove. Sabbath morning it commenced snowing, but not one meeting was suspended. About an inch of snow fell, and the air was piercing cold. Women with little children clustered about the stoves. It was touching to see one hundred and fifty people assembled for a . . . meeting under these circumstances. Some had come two hundred miles by private conveyance. . . .

"Sabbath morning I spoke encouraging words to those who had made so great an effort to attend the meeting. I told them that . . . our hopes are reaching forward to the Christian's summer, when we shall change climate, leave all the wintry blasts and fierce tempests behind, and to be taken to those mansions Jesus had gone to prepare for those who love Him." [5]

For the *Review and Herald,* Ellen wrote an account of visiting that camp meeting and included a portion of her Sabbath-morning talk. "This life at best is but the Christian's winter and the bleak winds of winter—disappointments, losses, pain, and anguish—are our lot here; but our hopes are reaching forward to the Christian's summer." Then she added these beautiful words in reference to Christ's coming: "We shall change climate . . . and be taken to those mansions Jesus has gone to prepare for those that love him." [6]

Ellen's talk revealed that she knew pain, disappointment, loss, and anguish all too well. She was urging the believers who attended camp meeting, through a vivid nature analogy, to hang on, to not give up hope when they, too, faced loss and anguish.

Now that we are on the subject of camp meeting, let's take a closer look into what it was like to attend camp meeting more than a century ago.

In 1878 Ellen and James were living in California. James was not feeling well and decided it was best for him to return to Battle Creek for treatment at the sanitarium. Ellen would stay in the West. She felt impressed to go to Oregon to attend camp meeting there. Very few Adventists lived in that area, and for her it was almost like going into unentered territory to expand the work of the Church. So they parted, James to the east, and Ellen to the northwest.

Finding that no railroads crossed the mountains between California and Oregon, she had to travel by ship. With other Adventists traveling to the Oregon camp meeting, Ellen boarded a steamship called the *Oregon* and sailed from San Francisco through the Golden Gate and then north.

The ship immediately entered rough water. And this is what she wrote about it. "I remained on deck after nearly all had abandoned it because of seasickness. I enjoyed the sight of the billows running mountain high, blue and green, and the dashing spray reflecting all the colors of the rainbow. I could not become weary of looking upon that grand scene."

Ellen was not afraid, because she knew she was going where God wanted her to go. She loved it. She didn't even want to go inside at night. "I continued on deck," she wrote. "The captain had provided me a deck chair, and blankets to serve as a protection from the chilly air. . . . The plunging waves were pitching our ship fearfully."

But as it became colder and colder, the captain insisted she go inside. She replied that she would rather get sick out on deck than to be sick in her cabin. As a compromise, the captain arranged for a stewardess to help Ellen into an upper saloon, where they placed a mattress on the floor—and immediately she became seasick.

Then when the ship finally entered the Columbia River, the water became calm. She wrote that it "was as smooth as glass." Ellen was helped out to the deck, where she met with "a beautiful morning, and the passengers poured out on deck like a swarm of bees."

Now let her tell you what happened when she went ashore. "When I walked up through the streets," Ellen wrote, "it seemed to me as though I was still on the boat, and I would step so high that people must have thought I was drunk."

Ellen went to Salem by train, but even though she had enjoyed her boat trip, except for the seasickness, it left her feeling weak. Yet, in spite of not feeling well, she did accept a few appointments to speak. Once she began, she was soon flooded with invitations to lecture in many towns and cities around Oregon. She said No to every one of them.

Her main reason for going to Oregon in the first place was to attend camp meeting—Oregon's first. And she did.

But what about her personal attitude as she faced all this? She wasn't feeling well, and it bothered her. "I miss James," she wrote, "oh, so much." Then she went on to add, "I . . . hope to be in good running order by camp meeting."

She was also worried, now that she was there, about how things would turn out. "I cannot sleep nights," she wrote. "My heart is drawn out in prayer to God for a fitness for the work." But she continued, "He will hear; He will answer. . . . I have not a doubt about it. Work!" she added, "I need not cross the plains [a trip across the United States] to find it. It is heaping up everywhere. But my work must be here on the coast till I get marching orders."

And once she saw the campground, she had these remarks. "Just at the entrance to the camp ground was a large tree, and they told us that that tree had been the place of the Indians' burying ground. Here they would lay their dead until they could take them away to some other spot."

The camp meeting began on June 27. The following night she asked this question: "Will there be souls saved as the result of this effort?" She had nothing to worry about, for God was in charge. And as the meetings continued, more and more people came. New tents were going up all the time, until two hundred campers were counted. And on the weekend, over two thousand people flooded the grounds. That camp meeting was a success. There had been no need for her to be concerned. But being the human that she was, she did feel moments of anxiety.

Ellen's return trip brought another difficulty. She had a hard time locating a ship to take her back to California. Most ships were booked in advance by tourists and carried between eight hundred and one thousand passengers. But, in time, Ellen did find a cabin for two on a ship called the *Idaho*. Her traveling companion was a teenager named Edith Donaldson, who was on her way to Battle Creek to attend college. After Edith was later baptized in Battle Creek, Ellen commented, "Here is another proof of the importance of Seventh-day Adventists' sending their children to our school."

On board the *Idaho* and in her lower-deck stateroom, Mrs. White asked to have the porthole opened. Not long afterward, a huge wave splashed a stream of water into the cabin, soaking everything. The steward came to their rescue, and he set things in order—also closing the porthole. Ellen lamented, "and thus ended the fresh air I was to have in my stateroom."

One bright spot stood out on their return voyage to San Francisco—again, something from nature. And as always, she wrote about it. "The word came that there is a school of whales in sight and I am called to see them. It is quite an interesting spectacle to see these monsters of the deep spouting the water high up from the ocean."[7]

In a few days Ellen was back on a train headed east to join up with James. Once more together, the two of them spent the rest of the summer traveling and speaking at one camp meeting after another.

The following year James and Ellen traveled to a camp meeting in Dakota Territory. Instead of suffering from seasickness, Ellen endured the discomfort of extreme heat and pesky mosquitoes.

Elder and Mrs. White traveled the last twenty-five miles of their journey by stagecoach. On July 14, 1879, Mrs. White wrote from Sioux Falls, Dakota Territory, "One hundred and fifty Sabbathkeepers camped on the ground. It is a beautiful encampment upon an island. The falls is within a few feet of the campground, and the fall of water is rather too distinctly heard.

"It is excessively hot. We are encamped in a grove belted with underbrush, which makes it impossible to get much air. It has seemed as though we should dissolve. . . . I must go upon the stand to speak. Yesterday, Sunday, I spoke to the crowd for one hour and a half. The people listened with great attention, although there was scarcely a breath of air stirring. My clothing was wet through."[8]

Mary K. White, Ellen's daughter-in-law, gave additional details. In it she said "that 15 tents were up, and several covered wagons. She described the heat and another problem, mosquitoes. 'They came ten thousand strong and pitched battle against us.' She also described the large slablike rocks, the clear river water, and told how the 'careworn elders in Israel indulged in cooling themselves in its silver spray nearly every day.' "[9]

"Travel" should have been Ellen White's middle name. She was always going somewhere. One would think she had wheels instead of feet. In addition to traveling across the United States many times to attend and speak at meetings, Ellen White traveled frequently during the approximately two years she lived in Europe.

When asked to visit northern Italy, her mind flashed to a sentence she had noticed in the *Review and Herald.* It read, "Come over into Italy and help us." She went.

And what did she find when she got there? Listen to this! She found many of the Waldensian people living in great poverty. In winter some of them moved into the stables with their animals for warmth. At the time of Mrs. White's visit, an Adventist worker was "holding Bible readings with the people in their stables. . . . The average attendance was from forty to fifty. There, on the dirt floor of the stable which was sometimes strewn with leaves or straw, or sitting on boards placed across boxes, these would sit and listen for an hour or two, and then would remain after the meeting closed to talk over what had been said."[10]

When Ellen traveled in Scandinavia, she found few suitable places to hold meetings. In Copenhagen, Denmark, she had to speak in a damp, unheated hall with a penetrating chill in the air, "that made one shiver in the warmest wrappings." There also she spoke in the basement of a building, in the upper stories of which were halls for dancing, and places for drinking.[11] In Stockholm, Sweden, Ellen reported, "There could not be found standing room for all who would come in. A crowd filled the aisle and around the door. They listened with the deepest interest. The hall was so densely packed one woman fainted. . . . Accommodations for places of meetings are not healthy or safe."[12]

In contrast, when she spoke in Christiania [now Oslo], Norway, sixteen hundred people came to hear Ellen's lecture on temperance. The meeting place was in the largest hall in the city, a military gymnasium.[13]

Why, one might ask, did Ellen White endure the inconvenience of frequent travel and numerous speaking appointments, along with the discomfort and weariness that went with it? The answer is simple. God had asked her to speak, and speak she did. She described the urgency she felt to share the message: "Talk it, pray it, sing it," she said, "fill the world with the message of His truth, and keep pressing on into the regions beyond."[14]

In an article from the *Review and Herald* during 1883, I discovered something written by Ellen that impressed me incredibly. It was only one sentence long. She was writing about the pioneers of the Adventist Church and of the hardships they endured. Many of those men and women, she wrote, were gone, but memories of them would always remain. Looking back, she summarized the early years of the Church: "Then," she said, "it cost everything to be a believer."[15]

---

1. Ellen G. White Estate, "Spirit of Prophecy Emphasis Week for Elementary Schools, 1965," 21.

2. Ibid., 31.

3. Ellen G. White, *The Health Reformer,* April 1, 1871.

4. Ellen G. White, *Child Guidance* (Nashville, Tenn,: Southern Publishing Association, 1954), 59.

5. Ellen G. White Estate, "Spirit of Prophecy Emphasis Week for Elementary Schools, 1971," 25.

6. *Review and Herald,* November 7, 1878.

7. Ellen G. White Estate, "Spirit of Prophecy Emphasis Week for Elementary Schools, 1972," 29-34.

8. Ellen G. White, *Manuscript Releases* (Silver Spring, Md.: E. G. White Estate, 1990), 5:191.

9. "Spirit of Prophecy Emphasis Week, 1972," 1.

10. *Historical Sketches,* 248.

11. Ibid., 182, 183.

12. Ellen G. White, *Manuscript Releases* (Silver Spring, Md.: E. G. White Estate, 1990), 3:373.

13. *Historical Sketches,* 207.

14. Ellen G. White, *Testimonies for the Church* (Nampa, Idaho: Pacific Press Publishing Assn., 1948), 9:30.

15. *Review and Herald,* November 20, 1883.

CHAPTER THREE

What the *Review* Remembers

I n the early years of their marriage, James referred to Ellen as "Mrs. W." Others did the same. Many examples of this are found on the pages of a publication called the *Review and Herald.*

The *Review and Herald* is important to Seventh-day Adventists because it is the denomination's official magazine. When James White released the first issue in November 1850, it carried the title of the *Second Advent Review and Sabbath Herald.* More than a century later, in 1961, the name was officially shortened to the *Review and Herald.* More recently, the name was changed to the *Adventist Review.* But over the years, most people refer to the magazine as the *Review.*

James White was the first editor of the *Review and Herald* magazine and held that position several times during the next thirty yeears. The early issues looked more like a newspaper than a magazine. During those decades, the publication usually carried a column that James White wrote himself. At times, it read like a diary, telling what he and Ellen had done each week. These columns make informative and fascinating reading.

Let's read from those early pages of the *Review*. From them we will learn more of what James and Ellen's life was like and about some of the issues the developing Church was facing during those years.

The late 1850s and on into the 1870s were critical times in the development of the Seventh-day Adventist Church. This early growth period could be called its childhood. The Great Disappointment of 1844 was past. Ellen White began to speak and write about the messages she had received in her visions. Response to the visions ranged from belief to indifference and outright opposition. Then there was the Sabbath question, a new concept for everyone. The future of the young Church rested in the hands of a very small group of people. There were many issues to contend with, even among the leaders, because not everything was clear to them. Take the matter of health reform, for instance. James White, on the pages of the *Review,* appealed to Church members to smoke their cigars outside of the building, not inside. He didn't ask them not to smoke, just do it outside. This, of course, changed later, when Ellen received additional information about health reform.

It's time now to see what we can learn about James and Ellen White as we open a few issues of the *Review*. Let's start with the April 14, 1868, issue.

It reads: "In 1847, while on our passage in a steamboat from Portland, Maine, to Boston, Mass., Mrs. W. was speaking to those around her in the ladies' cabin of the fearful storm we encountered in a recent passage between the two cities. She spoke of the importance of being always prepared for the close of our probation, either at death, or at the coming of Christ. A lady near her replied: 'That is the way the Millerites talk. I mean to have a jolly good time before

I become a long-faced Christian. The Millerites are the most de-luded set on earth. On the day they were expecting Christ to come, companies in different places put on their ascension robes, and went into graveyards, and upon the tops of houses and high hills, and there remained, praying and singing till the time passed by.'

"Mrs. W. then inquired of the lady if she saw any of these per-sons thus attired. She answered: 'No, I did not see them myself, but a friend who saw them told me. And the fact is so well understood everywhere, that I believe it as much as though I saw it myself.'

"At this point, another lady, feeling that the testimony of the first should not be questioned, stated: 'It is of no use to deny that the Millerites did put on ascension robes, for they did do it in towns all around where I live.'

"Mrs. W. asked this lady if she saw them with their robes on. She replied: 'No I did not see them, as they were not in my immediate neighborhood. But it was commonly reported, and generally believed, that they did make white linen ascension robes and put them on.'

"By this time strong feelings were evidently controlling these two ladies, because Mrs. W. did not seem to credit what they said against the Millerites. And the first in the conversation stated with emotions of excitement and passion: 'I know it was so. I fully believe the testimony of those who have told me these things. I believe what my friends have told me about those fanatical Mil-lerites, the same as though I saw it myself.'

"Mrs. W. then inquired of her for names of some persons who had figured in this fanatical movement. She stated that if the put-ting on of ascension robes was so very common, certainly she could give the names of some. To this she replied: 'Certainly I can give you names. There were the twin Harmon [Ellen White's maiden name] girls in Portland. My friends told me that they saw their robes, and saw them going out to the graveyard with them on. Since the time has passed, they have become infidels.'

"A school-mate of Mrs. W., who had never been an Adventist, was in that cabin, and had watched the conversation with mirthful interest. She had been acquainted with the Harmon girls during the entire period of their Second Advent experience. She could no longer restrain her feelings, and broke out in a laughing mood as she pointed to Mrs. W.

" 'This is one of those twin Harmon girls. I have known them always, and know that this report of their making and wearing ascension robes is all a lie. I never was a Millerite, and I do not believe that anything of the kind ever took place.'

"The storm that was fast arising in that cabin suddenly abated, and there followed a great calm. Mrs. W. then stated that all the stories about ascension robes were probably as destitute of truth as this one concerning the Harmon girls."[1]

In that same article, James White had this to say.

"Fifty dollars reward is offered to any person who will present unquestionable proofs of the truthfulness of these statements that believers in the second advent of Christ, on the day of expectation, did put on ascension robes. Those who can produce such proofs are requested to forward them immediately to the writer, at Greenville, Montcalm Co., Mich., and receive fifty dollars by the return of the mail."

No one ever collected the fifty dollars.

Now let's turn the pages in the same issue of the *Review* to an article written by Ellen herself. At the beginning of the article, there is a drawing of a woman in a short dress. That "short" dress is about six inches above the floor, and it shows the woman's shoes and ankles. This was shocking for that day and age. And to the total embarrassment of James White, Ellen promoted wearing that kind of dress. He felt that when she was wearing it and he was with her, people were staring at her and him too. He did not like the change. However, in an earlier issue of the *Review,* he did write about the dress. He recorded Ellen's cautions to women who wanted to wear the reform dress and her practical suggestions on how they should handle the situation if they faced negative reactions or opposition from doing so.

"She [Ellen White] teaches that it is the duty of all Christian women to adopt the reformed dress, with the exception of those cases where a rigid father or husband forbids it, causing a constant war which might be a greater detriment to health than an improper style of dress. . . . She says to all, 'Don't put on the short dress till you can put it on right.' "[2]

Now, back to the article that Ellen herself wrote, praising the reform dress and listing its merits. The article is quite long and in places very humorous. So, let's take a look at just a little of what she had to say about that wonderful shorter skirt.

In the beginning of her article, she listed the evils of the long skirt. Here is one from the list. "If she goes into the garden [wearing the long skirt] to walk or to work among the flowers, to share the early, refreshing, morning air, unless she holds them up [and there were several layers to hold up] with both hands, her skirts are dragging and drabbling in dirt and dew, until they are wet and muddy. Fashion attaches to her cloth that is, in this case, used as a sort of mop. This is exceedingly inconvenient. But for the sake of fashion it must be endured."

Later in the article, she explains how the reformed dress, with its shorter skirt, is more convenient and more healthful than a skirt that drags the ground, even if it is less fashionable. "True, it is not fashionable. But what of that? Fashions do not always come from Heaven. Neither do they always come from the pure, the virtuous, and the good."

And she didn't stop there; she had a lot more to say. "It is true that this style of dress exposes her feet. And why should she be ashamed of her well-clad feet any more than men are of theirs? It is of no use for her to try to conceal the fact that she has feet. This was a settled fact long before the use of trailing skirts extended by hoops, giving her the appearance of a hay stack, or a Dutch churn."

"Oh God," she said, "must this state of things continue?"

Ellen ended her article on the benefits of wearing the reformed dress with an exhortation. "Here comes the cross and the reproach, for simply doing right, in the face of the tyrant-Fashion. God help us to have the moral courage to do right, and to labor patiently and humbly in the great cause of reform."

And for her final remark, she signs off with this: "In behalf of my sisters who adopt the reform dress. Ellen G. White."[3]

James and Ellen both put their names to a short article appearing in the March 24, 1868, issue of the *Review*. The health message was still quite new among Adventists, and people had many questions. Along with other things, the article was concerned about the morality of church members raising hops. This shows that Ellen and James had many issues to handle, besides theology and church organization.

Let's read what they had to say.

"Hops. In answer to many inquiries, we would say that we believe there is business for Seventh-day Adventists to enter upon for a livelihood, more consistent with their faith than the raising of hops, tobacco, or swine.

"And we would recommend that they plant no more hops, or tobacco fields, and that they reduce the number of their swine. They may yet see it duty, as most consistent believers do, to keep no more. We would not urge this opinion upon any. Much less would we take the responsibility of saying, 'Plow up your hop and tobacco fields, and sacrifice your swine to the dogs.'

"While we would say to those who are disposed to crowd hop[s], tobacco, and swine growers among our people, that they have no right to make these things, in any sense, a test of Christian fellowship, we would also say to those who have these miserable things on hand, if you can get them off your hands without great loss, consistency with the faith of the people whose publications and oral teachings have so much to say on the subject of reform, more than suggests, that you should get them off your hands as soon as possible."[4]

Let's return to the subject of camp meetings again and see what we can learn about attending camp meetings from reading the *Review and Herald*. James did most of the reporting and had the feeling that church members across the country wanted to know what he and Ellen were doing. Because people wanted to see the Whites and hear them speak, they were in demand everywhere. And we must realize that travel in the 1800s was not like it is today. So with this in mind, we will turn back the clock and look at the August 5, 1875, issue.

Uriah Smith, the editor at that time, placed a general invitation to attend camp meeting in the August 5, 1875, issue. "Let there be a general rally. All bring tents who can. Those who cannot provide themselves with tents, should not fail to bring bedding, clothing, quilts, blankets, [and notice this] buffalo robes, etc. Room will be made for all."

That same issue carried these two notices about transportation. One was titled "Camp-meeting Tickets." It read, "The Michigan Central R. R. will grant round trip tickets at one fare from Kalamazoo and Jackson, and all points between, to those coming to our camp-meeting, Aug. 10 through 17. The Chicago and Lake Huron R. R. will also convey passengers to and from the meeting at half fare."

We also have this announcement titled "Stop at the Grounds." It read, "The accommodation and mail trains on the Michigan Central R. R. will stop at the campground, about one mile west of the station in the city, Aug 9 through 18."[5]

James White always had a lot to say about camp meetings. Here is one comment about the socializing going on at camp meeting that appeared in the *Review* for September 7, 1876. Remember, as you read, that he was sometimes very blunt and usually came right to the point. Here it is.

"Some of the sisterhood, not excepting old ladies, were decidedly gifted in talking about nothing in particular. When people will talk real sound common sense and religion, we say let them talk; but we confess our utter inability to enjoy hour after hour of common chatter, tinged with vulgar attempts at small wit. If there is anything that can be brought to camp-meeting which God hates, it is this cheap, driveling nonsense."[6]

Did this scolding make enemies? You be the judge.

In that same article, James reported about a Christian temperance meeting at which Ellen spoke. He commented that temperance was one of her favorite subjects. Officers from the local Temperance Association had asked her to speak in the city hall. They promised that a good crowd of at least a thousand people would attend. Now, speaking about his wife, James wrote the following.

"The strain of speaking twice on Sunday to the crowd had been great, and the reaction on Monday was inevitable, threatening a partial failure. But the temperance men were exceedingly urgent, and the risk was taken, and the appointment went out. And if cheers, and expressions of thanks, heavy amens, tears, smiles, and kisses from the fair temperance ladies at the close, are evident in the case, it was one of the good woman's best efforts."

Just how did Ellen handle that mixed crowd of non-Adventists? What did she tell them? James continues.

"She struck intemperance at the very root, showing that on the home table largely exists the fountain from which flow the first tiny rivulets of perverted appetite, which soon deepen into an uncontrollable current of indulgence and sweep the victim to a drunkard's grave. She arraigned the sin of mothers in giving so much time to the follies of dress instead of giving it to the moral and mental elevation of their household." She also went on to say that fathers wasted time, health, and money on their friends instead of training their children in how to distinguish between right and wrong.[7]

The Whites wore out quickly with their endless rounds of camp-meeting appointments, plus all the other work they had to do. And wouldn't you know it, James published comments about how he and Ellen were treated too. Read his complaints in the August 10, 1876, issue of the *Review.*

"Sometimes we are left to pitch our tent, when really too weary to stand, then to take the stand [speaker's platform] to speak; next are rushed into a business session, and then, after filling up each long day, from 5 a.m. to 9:30 p.m., to pack up, and take down the tent. The brethren are generally too busy or too thoughtless to assist. But when about to leave, when we wish to be left alone to complete arrangements for the train, then scores rush in to say a word, ask advice, or attend to some neglected business. These neglects and inconsistencies are fast wearing us out, and forcing us to be present at our camp-meetings but two days each at most."[8]

The old *Review* articles give numerous glimpses into James and Ellen White's lives. We can learn about people who irritated them, experiences that made them laugh, and church issues they had to deal with. But every article reveals their dedication to serving the Lord faithfully through nurturing and guiding the developing Seventh-day Adventist denomination.

---

1. *Review and Herald,* April 14, 1868.
2. Ibid., March 17, 1868.
3. Ibid., April 14, 1868.
4. Ibid., March 24, 1868.
5. Ibid., August 5, 1875.
6. Ibid., September 7, 1876.
7. Ibid.
8. Ibid., August 10, 1876.

CHAPTER FOUR

Fern Tree Gully

While browsing through a large flea market one day, I happened across a table displaying a number of old books. I deliberately looked away and said to myself, *I don't need any more books.* I could picture the shelves and shelves of books I had at home. I also had boxes filled with them. As I started to walk away, out of the corner of one eye I saw a book title that made me stop. It was *Mrs. Marco Polo Remembers.* Needless to say, I bought the book. After all, it was only a dollar. I also bought it because I knew that Mrs. Marco Polo could never have written that book. Later in the day, as I leafed through its pages, I discovered that the book was the journal of a woman who had made a trip through the Orient in 1908. It was a diary of her honeymoon.

Now, why should that book be of interest to me? It wasn't the honeymoon part that took my attention. Oh no! It was something else. What held my attention, besides the title, was a page that just happened to fall open as I leafed through the contents. The woman and her new husband were in Japan.

This is what I read. "Another day we took bamboo chairs, balanced precariously on the shoulders of four men, and started up a slender mountain trail that lay like a thread upon the hills."

She went on to add, "We plunged through a dark forest of bamboo growing thick and interlocking over our head." It must have been a wild and scary ride. But from the reading, I gathered that they enjoyed every minute of it.

And the trip back down the mountain must have been even more hair-raising. She described it this way: "The ground seethed and bubbled beneath our feet. Our men trotted so that, perched high in our chairs, we felt like passengers on a stormy sea."[1]

Now, why should a story like this be of interest to me in a book about Ellen White?

For an answer, let's jump ahead a few years from our previous chapter and travel down under to Australia. We go to the year 1892 and to a forest called Fern Tree Gully, about twenty-five miles from Melbourne, Australia.

As you read this, I want you to keep in mind a picture of that honeymoon couple as they were carried down a mountain in Japan. Remember how they hung on for dear life as they bumped and swayed in their sedan chairs. Remember, also, that even though the ride was scary, they loved every step their carriers took. It was exciting.

Hold that thought as we go to our story about Ellen White. It was December 29, 1892. In a little-known area of Australia grew one of nature's most beautiful gardens. Not many people traveled there in the late 1800s.

Some of Ellen White's friends were camping at Fern Tree Gully and were determined that Ellen should enjoy the beauty there too. But how to get her there was a problem. Fabulous and glorious as the forest was, Ellen knew her painful hip would never allow her to hike in to see Fern Tree Gully. There was undergrowth to struggle through and perhaps fallen trees to climb over. But Ellen did agree to take an excursion on the train to enjoy the scenery. She was suffering from a headache and realized that she probably would not be able to get any writing done anyway if she stayed home.

The train went within two miles of the site where a number of Ellen's church friends were camping. They had even arranged for a carriage to meet the train and take her the last two miles. There was nothing for her to worry about, they told her. It was all set, she was going.

So off Ellen went, not knowing of the wonderful things that lay in store for her. Because, in an unusual and totally unexpected way, one of God's surprises was soon to be hers.

More than thirty people were waiting at the campsite as her carriage came to a stop. A large canvas canopy had been set up and tablecloths were neatly spread on the ground beneath it. And the sun was shining through it, casting a golden glow on dishes filled with fresh-picked raspberries, potatoes, green beans, and rice pudding. She was delighted.

After the meal, it was time for their trip to see the great trees in Fern Tree Gully. Almost everyone went. Ellen followed along in a little two-wheeled carriage called a trap. But they soon had to stop, because the horse couldn't pull the trap any farther. The going was too rough.

At this point Ellen grew a little nervous. She didn't want to chance going into Fern Gully because she knew she could never walk through the heavy growth. "I did not favor this," was her comment.

Ellen never noticed, but when they were eating their meal at the camp, a man named Mr. Faulkhead had slipped away. He went off looking for a certain type of chair, which he finally located two miles away. Once this was done, the men cut a few strong poles from nearby trees and tied them to the chair. It was a make-shift sedan chair, not unlike the ones our honeymooners had traveled in.

Ellen tried it out as Mr. Faulkhead and Mr. Prismall lifted the chair. She hung on as tight as she could, and as she said later, they "bore me along."

And so it went. "I [was] unwilling to burden them," she wrote, and they "determined to persevere—over logs, fallen trees, and narrow passages cut between trees by Byron Belden and his father."

Ellen had to grip the chair tightly in a few places. "Sometimes," she said, "it required four men to keep the chair conveyance in safety." This was especially true when they climbed over fallen trees or broke through thick brush.

Did she enjoy the trip? "It was a marvelous passage," she wrote, "seated in my chair with human charioteers to take me over the road." She loved it.

"We came to a level spot," she continued to relate, "in Fern Gully, and tarried awhile." I am sure the men needed the rest. Ellen was not a light person to carry.

She continues about the trip. "There were trees in every form and of various dimensions and heights, and the burden of nature was the perfect, beautiful ferns growing from the top of these fern trees. One tree stood out in distinctive beauty of perfection from all others. The formation of the ferns upon the top of this tree, about twenty feet in height, was more perfect than anything we afterwards had the privilege of seeing. I delight to carry in my mind this model of nature's perfection in Fern Tree Gully. It is a beautiful specimen of the Lord's work in its natural state. Surrounding it were fern trees of large growth, but this tree was a crown or circular in form, and in beautiful exactitude and order, so fresh in foliage of deep green, that I was assured in my own mind it could not be excelled."

At this point of the trip, a decision had to be made. She wrote: "Now we had not reached the dense growth and the question was, Should we go forward or return?"

The men carrying the chair wanted to go on, but Ellen was happy with what she had already enjoyed. "I was perfectly satisfied with what I had already seen. I could take the picture and preserve it in my mind—one fern tree so perfect in form amid a vast number that were of uncouth proportions and wanting in perfection in fern tree loveliness."

So what did they do? Did they continue on, or had they seen enough and turned back? Let her tell it.

"The brethren were not satisfied unless they took me the whole way, so on they went, in most inaccessible paths, until the journey was complete, and I stood under the shadow of the fern trees in the gully. There were the large trees covered with growing ferns, and it was very interesting to see the great height of the trees and their varied formation and manner of growth. There were revealed that young saplings had fastened themselves to the trunk of the fern tree and became one with it, growing into the tree and presenting entirely a different tree than the fern. Both were growing together. It was impossible to separate the one from the other unless the fern were much cut to pieces."

She continued. "After viewing this wonderful production of nature as long as we thought safe, for it was quite damp in the forest of ferns, my bearers took up their burden, made their way to open ground, passed down the hill of thick, matted grass—a much shorter route than we came. We were not long descending the hill, and I gave my hearty thanks to those who were so full of perseverance to carry out the plans of their devising to have Sister White see Fern Tree Gully. I know they must be very tired, having carried me to the gully and back, no less than three miles."

Ellen typically enjoyed finding spiritual lessons in her observations of nature. Her trip to Fern Tree Gully was no exception. "The church," she said, "may be compared to the growth of trees. Many of the fern trees grow in awkward, unlovely positions. Some gather to themselves the properties of the earth, which they appropriate to fern tree life, in beauty and strength and perfection. Others were bending sideways, unable to stand erect. In others, the fern boughs were imperfect, irregular, wanting in perfection of form and maturity. Thus it is with church members, in formation of Christian character. Some do not appropriate to themselves the precious promises of God, and the provisions made at infinite cost to Heaven that divine power might combine with human effort, that all that is evil should be discarded and overcome, and through faith in Jesus Christ, through watchfulness and prayer, they might be partakers of the divine nature, having escaped the corruption that is in the world through lust."[2]

So there we have the story of a group of loving friends from the church wanting to share the wonders of nature with the little lady who meant so much to them. They went all out to give her a special treat and make her happy. They were well aware of the hardships she was going through, and they just wanted her to have a little time off for contentment and joy. They wanted her to know that they really cared about her. These people went the extra mile for someone they had grown to love and admire in that great land down under called Australia.

1. Mary Parker Dunning, *Mrs. Marco Polo Remembers* (Boston: Houghton Mifflin Company, 1968), 13.
2. Ellen G. White, *Manuscript Releases* (Silver Spring, Md.: E. G. White Estate, 1990), 8:51-55.

CHAPTER FIVE

"Never Write Failure"

A winding stairway connects the first and second floors of the house I lived in for a number of years. It is situated next to three large windows. On the other side of this staircase is a spacious entryway. It also has three huge windows that allow a view from the opposite side of the house. If one were to stand on the stairway and gaze through any one of these six windows, miles of Idaho countryside would open in either direction.

One morning while living there, I was walking down that stairway in a discouraged mood. I was upset over something that had gone wrong, which completely stressed me out. I had made up my mind that in no way was I going to be happy. I stopped halfway down the stairs because I thought I saw something move in a field behind the house. A cat, I presumed. There definitely was something out there near my back fence. And when I finally recognized what it was, I couldn't believe my eyes. I blinked, rubbed my eyes, and looked again. Yes, it was still there. I was looking at a pure-white pheasant. I had never heard of such a thing. It was a wonder to behold. Its head was held high, and its snow-white tail feathers trailed out behind it. The body was sleek and graceful. I just could not believe what I was seeing. *But,* I wondered, *was it really a pheasant?* Yes it was, because a few feet behind it walked a beautiful male. Its feathers were brilliantly colored like all the other pheasants I had seen. I almost held my breath until both vanished into clumps of tall grass.

My gloomy, discouraged attitude changed instantly. Then I thought back to a few minutes before I had started down the stairs. I had prayed. I had given my day over to God—then completely forgotten about it. But He hadn't.

I was living for myself, depending entirely upon me to control my new day and life. But when I had walked down those stairs and stopped to look through a window, God gave me a gift to remind me that I had asked Him—not me—to be in charge of my life. And just as a reminder, He gave me a beautiful picture of His love and care by letting me see the rare white pheasant. The pheasants were not concerned about their day or where it would take them; He was watching over them. They just went about doing what pheasants do. There was no stress. And when I realized this, I knew the Lord was telling me that He was doing the same thing for me. It is a lesson I will never forget.

Was Ellen ever depressed? Leaders are almost always criticized for things they either do or fail to do. Did Ellen respond to criticism with discouragement? Did she have to learn how to trust, learn how to feel joyful? Let's find out.

She wrote in her diary for Friday, June 3, 1859, the following entry. "A number [of people] came from Monterey [Michigan] and stopped with us. Am sorry that I cannot enjoy their company. I have no health and my mind is completely depressed."

On June 4 she wrote, "Was very sick and much discouraged. Unable to attend meeting." She also mentioned that around midnight on June 4, her sickness worried her so much that she felt she would die. She fainted at the thought. Her diary reads, "Andrews and Loughborough were sent for."

The men prayed. And God answered their sincere prayers immediately. Ellen wrote about it. "The depression, the heavy weight, was lifted from my aching heart. . . . I saw . . . that Satan had been trying to drive me to discouragement and despair, to make me desire death rather than life."[1]

Keeping her response in mind, let's leap ahead to the year 1911—late in Ellen's life—and read what Arthur White, her grandson, had to say about Ellen and discouragement. "Ellen White," he wrote, "understood so well the issues and the bountiful provisions for salvation that there was no place in her mind for discouragement."[2]

What happened here? How were her personality and attitude seemingly reversed?

I believe that she gradually came to understand that Satan is frequently the cause of depression and discouragement. But she was not fully aware of the source of her depression when she was a young woman in 1859. It took years and an ever-deepening friendship with Jesus to reveal to her that Satan was, and still is, the frequent source of depression. As her walk with Jesus became closer, her depression and discouragement disappeared. He was then her safeguard against negative thoughts and emotions.

Let's look at a couple situations illustrating the types of unfair criticism Ellen faced. She understood that Satan was attempting to discourage her through criticism. "Many professing Christians have become the agents of Satan, who uses them to criticize and to discourage nigh unto death those whom God has appointed to do a most important work."[3]

The first story is incomplete because Ellen White never told how she handled the situation. I don't believe she wanted us to have that information.

Here is the story as I found it.

"Sometimes it seemed to Mrs. White that whatever she did or didn't do, displeased somebody. She was used to criticism—but it always hurt. One time she was staying in a private home, helping with a tent meeting. The workers were wearing themselves out distributing handbills, meeting people and urging them to come to the evening meetings, then conducting them at the end of strenuous days. Some of the church people helped, but not all. Among this group was one lady who, Mrs. White wrote, 'was so overbearing that they could hardly live with her.' " Bossy and critical, she made life miserable for everybody. Mrs. White went out of her way to be gracious to the lady, but had little success.

"But the lady had a problem with Ellen White. She couldn't find anything to criticize! As the days went by and it was nearly time for the meetings to end, she became almost frantic. Finally she decided to go right through Mrs. White's trunk to try to find an extra bit of lace trim, or some ornamental buttons, or perhaps an expensive piece of satin ribbon, or a decorated hat, or something to criticize! She waited until she thought Mrs. White was gone for the evening, then tiptoed into the guest room, opened the visitor's trunk and started carefully taking out and inspecting every garment. Just when she was in the middle of it all, kneeling on the floor with piles of clothes all around her, in walked God's messenger, Ellen G. White!

"The story ends right here. We don't know who spoke first or what anybody said. But Mrs. White did make the remark when telling the story, 'We shall ever have just such people to deal with in this world. . . . It is a marvel to me what patience the Lord has with such crooked material.' "[4]

Ellen didn't reveal how that encounter ended. But her comments elsewhere reveal her attitude about criticism. "If all would refuse to hear evil of their neighbor, the talebearer would soon seek other employment. . . .

"God does not want any one person to be conscience for another. Talk of the love and humility of Jesus; but do not encourage the brethren and sisters to engage in picking flaws in the dress or appearance of one another. Some take delight in this work. . . . God would have them step down from the judgment seat; for He has never placed them there."[5]

Another incident that reveals how Ellen White responded to criticism involved a group of teenage boys. They had gone to a camp meeting only because their parents took them. They did not want to be there. They were loud and noisy on the grounds and openly rude during meetings. The boys laughed and made fun of the speakers, especially Ellen White. Yet, even as they were acting like this, they couldn't help listening to what she had to say.

One of the boys had an idea. He thought of taking Ellen's words and using them against her. She had talked about simplicity, especially when it came to dress. They had noticed that while she was speaking, Ellen had a gold watch pinned to her dress.

The boy said to his friend, " 'That means she's preaching one thing and practicing another.'

" 'Let's ask her about it. . . . I think we've really got her cornered this time, wearing a gold watch and telling the people to be so plain and self-sacrificing!'

"So, looking very innocent, the two walked up to Mrs. White as she was hurrying from one appointment to another. She was just coming from a meeting where prayer had been offered for these unconverted young people.

" 'Mrs. White, may we ask you a question?' asked the bolder one.

" 'Certainly,' she answered politely.

" 'We've been listening to your sermons and they are very interesting. But some people are troubled because you don't practice what you preach.'

"Mrs. White seemed surprised. 'What do you mean?' she asked.

" 'Well, that watch,' he answered, pointing to the small timepiece she had pinned to her dress as was the custom in those days. 'You say we shouldn't wear gold, and the Bible says it too, but how about that gold watch of yours? People are saying that that watch proves you don't really believe what you are asking them to do.'

"Amazed, Mrs. White looked down at the offending watch. She later told how she happened to have it. 'Some time before, I had received a present of a little open-faced, gold watch. It was very ancient in appearance, and certainly never would have been worn for its beauty. I carried it because it was a good timepiece.'

"She may have recognized those two boys as being members of the trouble-making gang, but she simply told them that she would take care of the situation and went on her way. The young men ran to tell their friends, 'We really caught her this time!'

"What did she do about it? She tells us: 'In order to avoid all occasion for any to stumble, I sold the watch.' Really, she didn't need to do that, just to satisfy her critics. The watch was old, not beautiful, and she certainly needed a timepiece. But Mrs. White didn't want anybody to stumble over anything they might see in her life."[6]

Ellen's mature understanding of how to overcome depression and discouragement is revealed in the following statement: "When discouragement comes, remember that the Lord's hosts are back of us. Remember that your strength is not found in words of discouragement. Remember that heaven is not lessened of any of its angels. These angels are just as ready to come to the help of God's people today as in the days of ancient Israel."[7]

In a 1912 letter to her son Edson, Ellen wrote, "Never write failure."[8]

Sara McEnterfer was Ellen's nurse and traveling companion for many years. About two years before Ellen died, Sara McEnterfer wrote to Ellen's son Willie about Ellen's cheerfulness. "She sings in the night and she sings in the day (even in the bathtub)."[9]

Ellen's refusal to give in to discouragement is further illustrated in how she responded to an illness in 1911. In the middle of March of that year she began treatments at the St. Helena Sanitarium for a condition suspected to be skin cancer.

"For several weeks I took treatment with the X-ray for the black spot that was on my forehead. In all I took twenty-three treatments, and these succeeded in entirely removing the mark. For this I am very grateful."[10] And that was all she had to say about it. She took the available medical treatment and left the result in God's care. She was not overly concerned about the outcome. Her motto, Never Write Failure, was illustrated again.

On Sabbath, February 13, 1915, Ellen tripped and fell as she entered her study. Her hip was broken. She was eighty-eight years old and did not recover from this accident.

How did she respond to the accident and the suffering that followed?

We have this report from her son Willie. "Since her accident she has told me that she feels that her work is done, her battles ended, and that she is willing to lie down and sleep till the resurrection morning, unless there is yet some special work the Lord has for her to do."

Ellen's keen sense of humor showed even during her final illness. Her appetite was failing, and she just did not feel like eating.

Sara McEnterfer was coaxing her to eat something. "Well, Sara," Ellen said, "I would not want to die before my time by overeating."[11]

Even Ellen's last words were words of courage quoted from 2 Timothy 1:12, "I know whom I have believed."[12]

---

1. Arthur L. White, *Ellen G. White: The Early Years, 1827-1862* (Hagerstown, Md.: Review and Herald Publishing Association, 1985), 406, 407.

2. Arthur L. White, *The Later Elmshaven Years, 1905-1915* (Hagerstown, Md.: Review and Herald Publishing Association, 1982), 339.

3. Ellen G. White, *Medical Ministry* (Nampa, Idaho: Pacific Press Publishing Association, 1963), 138.

4. Ellen G. White Estate, "Spirit of Prophecy Emphasis Week for Seventh-day Adventist Schools, 1972," 38, 39,

5. *Historical Sketches,* pp. 122, 123.

6. "Spirit of Prophecy Emphasis Week, 1972," 36-38.

7. *Record of Progress and An Earnest Appeal in Behalf of the Boulder Colorado Sanitarium,* 42.

8. *The Later Elmshaven Years,* 377.

9. Ibid., 393.

10. Ibid., 344.

11. Ibid., 425.

12. Ibid., 431.

CHAPTER SIX

What Happened on the River?

In the small town of Allegan, Michigan, a man was building a boat. The year was 1894. It didn't look much like a boat suitable for that area of the United States. Most of the boats around there were small and for fishing. But not this one; it was different. It looked more like a flat-bottomed barge with a small house on top. It also had a large deck. When it was finally finished, the boat was launched into the Kalamazoo River. It slowly made its way down "the crookedest river I ever saw," said its builder, Edson White. It was "full of snags and sand bars and logs and treetops." Edson and his wife, Emma, were on their way to Lake Michigan. "Outside of a few bruises to the upper works of the boat," he said, "it sustained no damage."[1]

At Douglas, the Kalamazoo entered Lake Michigan. From there they were towed across the lower part of the lake by a large fruit steamer.

What was this all about, and where were they going?

It happened twenty-nine years after the American Civil War.

Edson, who was forty-four years old at the time, had read one of his mother's writings about work that needed to be done in the South for the freed slaves. But no one in the Adventist denomination was doing anything to help them. One sentence in her writing hit Edson hard. "Sin rests upon us as a church because we have not made greater efforts for the salvation of souls among the colored people."

He was startled by this statement and said to himself, *Why don't we do something?* This was followed by *Why don't I do something?* He talked it over with his wife, Emma, and she agreed that they should do something about it together. So they built a boat and called it *The Morning Star*. Edson had, in the meantime, become a qualified river pilot.

Reaching the western shore of Lake Michigan, they soon entered the Mississippi River. They then sailed south for 1,500 miles. On January 10, 1895, they and a few people who had gone with them, reached Vicksburg, Mississippi. And their work began.

They were so successful that in one year's time a small group of blacks had joined the church, and more were coming all the time.

Bringing these former slaves and their families into the church was not Edson and Emma's only aim. They also began a school. These people needed to know how to read and write. The school was quite a sight to see. It wasn't only for children. "Middle-aged people came, and older ones too, all eager to learn to read and write." In time, so many came to their school-boat that night sessions were started. The first night thirty-five people showed up. Ten nights later there were 112. Then there were 133, and Edson had to build more benches. He said they sat "on seats which should have no more than four," but "we crowded from six to eight."

More than anything else, the students all wanted to learn to write. It wasn't easy teaching so many students at one time. The teacher wrote on a blackboard, and the students copied what he wrote. "On the front seats, where there can be no desks arranged, some sat on the floor and used the seat for a desk, and . . . several of the boys took their papers on their books and lay flat on the pulpit floor . . . and in this position did the best to learn to write."

Reading, spelling, arithmetic, penmanship, and grammar were taught on Monday and Thursday nights. The ages of the students were all the way from small children to grandmothers and grand-fathers.

Several young men asked for a Bible class. Edson taught this class after school hours. In time, some from this group continued their education and became Adventist preachers and teachers.

There was a small printing press on the boat. This allowed them to print handbills, advertising religious meetings were to be held aboard *The Morning Star* every Sunday afternoon. The hand-bills were scattered all over Vicksburg. The meetings turned out to be a great success. People loved the music. After more teachers and workers came to help Edson and Emma, they formed an or-chestra. "There was an organ and two cornets, one playing the melody, the other the alto." Edson wrote this to his brother, "You ought to see how they enjoy the singing!

"An elderly ex-slave, referred to as 'Antie Miller' said, 'I learned to read at White's school. In a month I could read, but I couldn't understand. I used to cry over it, but, then Sister White [Emma]—she'd encourage me. Come sit right down by me, she would, and help me. And in two months I could read so I could understand. Sister White certainly could sing. Brother White and she certainly could sing! She was the *best* singer!' "

But not everything went well. Some white people in the South still smarted from being defeated in the Civil War. They didn't like what the people on *The Morning Star* were doing. White people teaching blacks made them angry. Trouble was on the way.

One day "a mob came onto the boat and told [Edson] White to get out or they would hang him." Edson knew they meant every word they said. So, what did he do? He simply pulled up anchor and sailed to another place.

At Yazoo City, one of Edson's helpers, a man named Rogers, who lived in the city, was threatened. "You get out by five o'clock or you hang."

What happened? "He went to the mayor, who promised to send policemen to guard his home. Then," wrote Rogers, "that evening as we sat in our house, about seven o'clock there came a rap on the back door. My wife went to open it; we thought the mob had come. But it was a Negro who had come to warn us that the mob had come to the chapel. There were Negroes lying all around our house, armed, though we did not know it till afterwards. The mob searched every house in the Negro quarters to find us. . . . Then the mob started to burn the chapel. They found some cotton heaped up on the porch of one of the cabins nearby, and this they piled at the rear of the chapel, under the floor, poured coal oil over it and set it afire. When the flames shot up and were burning as high as the roof, they rode off whooping. The Negroes who stood around about watching said that as soon as the men had gone, the flames were smitten down as though by a hand, and died out of themselves. From this circumstance the school came to be known thereafter in all that country around about as 'The Holy School.'

"The next day was Sabbath, and in the morning my wife and I went over to hold Sabbath School. At first not a child nor women nor man would join us; they just stared at us awe-struck as we passed. But we finally induced a few of the more daring to come with us. And we held Sunday school the next day."

But trouble did not stop after that miracle. It continued.

"Another evening six white men shot at Mr. Rogers as he was trying to escape them. Two bullets whistled through his hat and knocked it off, but he was unhurt. At home he found his wife on her knees, praying for his safety. She had neither seen the mob nor heard the shots, but she feared that her husband was in danger."

So the work went on. And in just a few years, fifty such schools were operating along the rivers of the South, all under the protection and blessing of God.

While all of this was going on, Ellen, who was in Australia, wrote many letters encouraging Edson and Emma in their work. And when she finally returned to the United States, she traveled with them on the river for nearly a week with both her sons and Emma.

During the trip Ellen took on *The Morning Star,* it was decided that the new struggling Oakwood Manual Training School in Huntsville, Alabama, was to be enlarged and strengthened. It was at Oakwood also, in the early 1900s, where black ministers, teachers, and medical workers were being trained. Property was also purchased near Edgefield Junction, where the Madison School and Hospital would be built.

In a letter dated 1902, Ellen wrote about her feelings concerning her son's work for the black people of the South. "The pioneers of successful work among the colored people were obliged to teach old and young how to read. . . . They had to provide food and clothing for the needy. They had to speak comforting words to the downcast. Those who, after a day's work, walked miles to attend night school, needed sympathy. The teachers had to adapt their instruction to many varied minds.

"Angels of God looked on with approval. The workers had God's commendation. . . . They had passed through an experience of disappointment and trial. But Christian love and patience won for them the victory."

Ellen passed on to her son Edson and his wife, Emma, her understanding that "all are God's children. Through her life and her writings the Lord clearly revealed that there is no difference in His sight between black, white, brown, yellow or red."

Ellen wrote: "The religion of the Bible recognizes no cast or color. It ignores rank, wealth, worldly honor. God estimates men as men [and women as women]. With Him, character decides their worth. And we are to recognize the spirit of Christ in whoever it is revealed, be it white man or black."[2]

Finally, she gave this assurance: "You are not accountable for the color of your skin. And it does not in any way affect the question of your salvation. Your words are of far more consequence with God."[3]

---

1. This entire chapter is based on material found in Ellen G. White Estate, "Spirit of Prophecy Emphasis Week for Seventh-day Adventist Schools, 1974," 32-37.

2. Ellen G. White, *Testimonies for the Church* (Nampa, Idaho: Pacific Press, 1948), 9:223.

3. Ellen G. White, *Manuscript Releases* (Silver Spring, Md.: Ellen G. White Estate, 1990) 4:101.

CHAPTER SEVEN

"Our Dear Friend"

I
t should not surprise anyone that the highlight of Ellen White's week was the Sabbath. It was the same with Jesus.

In Mark 2:23-28, we find Jesus with His disciples. Here is what happened. "On a Sabbath day as Jesus and his disciples were walking through the fields, the disciples were breaking off heads of wheat and eating the grain.

"Some of the Jewish religious leaders said to Jesus, 'They shouldn't be doing that! It's against our laws to work by harvesting grain on the Sabbath.'

"But Jesus replied, 'Didn't you ever hear about the time King David and his companions were hungry, and he went into the house of God—Abiathar was High Priest then—and they ate the special bread only priests were allowed to eat? That was against the law too. But the Sabbath was made to benefit man, and not man to benefit the Sabbath. And I, the Messiah, have authority even to decide what men can do on Sabbath days!'" (TLB).

Verse 26 of the Revised Standard Version says that David and his men ate the "bread of the Presence," which was only to be eaten by the priests. Then in verse 27 it says this: " 'The sabbath was made for man, not man made for the sabbath.' " And the passage ends with verse 28: " 'So the Son of man is lord even of the sabbath.' "

Why have I quoted these verses? Let's find out.

Years ago, when I was a teenager living in Detroit, Michigan, I became a member of the Seventh-day Adventist Church. My family and I lived in the suburbs. It was miles and miles away from the Detroit Grand River Church, where I was a member. My sister and I would ride a bus to the city limits, where we would transfer to a city streetcar. It took hours and several more transfers before we arrived at the church. We made this trip every Sabbath. Mother went with us most of the time. And on rare occasions a church member would offer us a ride all the way to the church. But that was not usually the case.

Friends usually drove Mother home after church. But my sister and I would stay. We carried a lunch with us to make a day of it because of an afternoon meeting for the youth of the church. So, between lunchtime and the meeting, we had time on our hands. Groups of us would take walks together in the city or stop and talk in a park.

One Sabbath as we were passing an ice-cream parlor, which we called those places back then, we noticed a small boy coming out of the store. There was a smile on his face and a huge ice-cream cone in his hand. But just as he passed us, the ice cream fell out of the cone and plopped to the sidewalk. He began to cry as we all stood and watched. All, that is, except for one older person in our group. As we watched the crying child, she quickly walked over to him, took him by the hand, and led him back into the store. They emerged in a few minutes. The boy was all smiles again, and in his hand was an ice-cream cone that was even bigger than the one he had dropped. He went happily on his way and we went ours.

This event bothered me for years. I was a new Adventist at the time—and young. I had been taught that doing secular business, including shopping, was breaking the Sabbath. Much later, I came to understand what I had really witnessed. I had watched a loving and caring demonstration of the Sabbath being made for people, and not people for the Sabbath.

We can learn a lot about joyful Sabbath keeping by finding out how Ellen White kept the Sabbath.

"During her thirty-four years of widowhood, Ellen White loved to think back to the days when she and her husband James had kept God's Sabbath together, of the many times they had bowed in prayer at the beginning and the close of His Holy day, described by Elder White as 'our dear friend, the blessed Sabbath.' He had often spoken of how important it is to guard 'both ends of it' and how 'upon our knees we should part with the Sabbath as with a very dear friend.' "[1]

Ellen prepared for Sabbaths during the week, especially when the White home was full of family and friends. She and James took care of many children in need of a home and spoke of them as being "adopted," though none legally took the family name. Let's read her description of those Sabbaths.

"When my children were small we had a large family of adopted children. We would have our work away [finished] before the setting of the sun. The children would hail the Sabbath as a joy. They would say, 'Now father and mother will give us some of their time.' We would take them out for a walk. We would take the Bible and some religious instruction to read to them, and explain to them the Scriptures. We would keep praying that they should know the truth of God's word. We would not lie abed Sabbath mornings because it was Sabbath. We would have our preparations all ready the day before so that we could go to service [church] without the hurry and worry. We would not stroll off and have a nice time to ourselves. We wanted our children to have all the privileges and blessings of God's sanctified rest day."[2]

Not long ago a vast section of the American Southwest was known as The Great American Desert. It covered several states— Arizona, Utah, Nevada, and New Mexico.

Let's go to Friday, December 12, 1884. In the distance we notice a thin dark line moving slowly across that desert. What is it? Drawing closer, we see the shape of a train. From a distance it appears to be a toy. But it isn't. It is real.

But this is no ordinary train. It's a special slowly moving freight pulling a couple of passenger coaches behind it. Those coaches were known as "emigrant cars." The trip would take longer than regular passenger-train travel, but the fare was cheaper. In her diary, Ellen described riding in the emigrant cars: "We eat and drink dust."[3]

Miles ahead, on the far horizon, the giant circle of the sun appears to grow larger and larger. Its flaming disc is slowly sinking from sight. But as it disappears, a shower of soft light turns everything it touches to wondrous shades of gold. Train rails glisten. Mountains turn soft red. Even the black smoke from the moving train begins to glow. Its unbroken trail floats for miles across sagebrush and sand, only to grow weaker and smaller, before disappearing forever.

Aboard that slow train sit Ellen White and a group of her friends. They are on their way to California. The day before, they had gone sightseeing in Santa Fe, New Mexico. Earlier on Friday, the train had stopped in Holbrook, Arizona, where some of the travelers visited a petrified forest. Now it is late Friday evening, and Sabbath is about to begin. Their journey will last until Sunday. Let's find out how Ellen and her friends observed the Sabbath on the train.

Ellen sits alone by a window, beginning Sabbath worship with prayer. Writing later about that traveling chapel on wheels, Ellen said, "The Lord drew very near by His Holy Spirit." She also added that they, "could go to rest without fear of accident or harm."

The train made very slow progress as it began to climb into the western mountains.

Sabbath morning found them high in the mountains, "hemmed in by the snow." "We saw," she wrote, "many workmen with their shovels on their shoulders returning from their work, having spent the night in clearing the track."

But Ellen and her friends were not the only passengers in those emigrant cars. Others aboard that train were affected by what they saw and heard from the Adventists.

"Some [passengers] had attended the meetings held every morning and evening during that tiresome journey, and on Sabbath they listened to an excellent Bible reading. Some who were not of our faith took part in this exercise, and seemed much interested. . . . This revival meeting," continued Ellen White, "on the cars en route for California was a deeply impressive scene, such a one as I never before witnessed."

Ellen's final comment about that train trip was this: "On Sunday, December 14, the weary emigrants reached their destination—California."[4]

A week earlier, Ellen had begun the first leg of that train trip to California, leaving on Friday, December 5, from Battle Creek. That Friday she traveled only as far as Chicago because Ellen avoided traveling on the Sabbath day whenever possible. In Chicago she attended services held at the Seventh-day Adventist Mission, a facility that Adventists no longer own today. She was glad she did so, because on that day she saw an elderly man, a son of William Miller, accept the Seventh-day Sabbath.

That afternoon in Chicago, she attended a meeting at the Scandinavian Church. The singing was in both English and Danish, but the guest speaker preached in English with no translation. "Some who had not been in this country long could understand but little; but they felt and enjoyed the spirit of the meeting." Although Ellen knew no Danish, she was pleased and thankful she spent that Sabbath in worship instead of riding west on a train. It was a delightful interruption to her travel.[5]

Sometimes Ellen White had the opportunity to provide hospitality and fellowship on Sabbath instead of receiving it. One delightful example took place in 1898, while Ellen was living in Australia.

A week of prayer was planned at the new school that had been started near her home. Ellen knew the students would attend the meetings—they weren't her immediate concern. Other people were on her mind. She had many new friends in the Cooranbong area where she lived, and she wanted them to be able to attend the special meetings. But many of them could not come because of distance and lack of transportation. They couldn't walk to the meetings from their farms and settlements. They were too far away. And many of the people had small children. So what did she do? She sent two of her own wagons and teams of horses to provide transportation for them. And when her friends reached the body of water called Dora Creek, she had a rowboat waiting to take them across.

Ellen knew that some of the Sunday-keeping visitors would take notice of one of the Adventist nurses working with a sick family. So that the visitors wouldn't be confused by seeing the nurses work on Sabbaths, she simply told them, "We believed that one of our sisters who was nursing a sick family was keeping the

Sabbath as much as the one who was leading a division of the Sabbath-school."

Ellen did more than provide transportation; her hospitality included lunch. At the close of the service the visitors were hungry. Word had been sent out that all should bring their own food, but Mrs. White didn't want anyone to miss dinner. "Knowing that the notice was short," she wrote, "and that some might come without lunch, we had provided abundance of plain food; and after some had been invited to the homes of our people, there were about forty who gathered under the broad-spreading gum trees, and ate their food with thanksgiving and friendly conversation."

And the hospitality continued. After sundown and Sabbath had ended, Ellen again had the rowboat, her wagons and teams of horses, ready to take the visitors home.[6] "They had much to talk about of what they had seen and heard that day, of how kindly they had been entertained, and of how Mrs. White and the school family had gone out of their way to provide food and transportation, even though it had been their Sabbath!"[7]

This reminds us of the time when Jesus fed several thousand people who had followed Him to a remote area to listen to His teaching.

We need to digress briefly with a little anecdote about the teams of horses that had provided transportation to the special Sabbath meeting. When Ellen sold her home in Australia, the buyer bought house and furnishings alike. Two of the horses went with the property. But Ellen's sense of humor is revealed when we learn the fate of the other team of horses. "Mrs. White gave her favorite driving horses, Jessie White and Jessie Haskell, to friends." Did you get that? She had given her horses second names—her own family name and the name of another Adventist pioneer worker in Australia.[8]

When living in California and working for the Pacific Press, I usually made one or more trips to Michigan every year. My purpose for doing this was to bring my mother and father west to spend winters with me. The climate was much better for them in California—and besides that, we enjoyed taking those trips together. I usually flew east then returned west with them and their car.

I remember one year especially as we were traveling through New Mexico. There was nothing for miles and miles but empty roads and desert. Suddenly, out in nowhere, we were surrounded by people. There were hundreds of them. But where did they come from? We didn't know. The road was blocked. We couldn't drive ahead, and certainly didn't want to turn around and go back.

We soon learned that a rodeo or some kind of festival was going on. And people came from miles around to attend. I finally realized that we had caught up to the tail end of a parade. So, with no other way of getting through town, Mother, Dad, and I joined the parade. It was great fun as we waved to the people. We didn't know them, and they didn't know us—but that was all right. We had just gotten started as part of the parade when someone poked his head into one of our car's open windows. It was a clown. "Here are your free tickets!" he said. I tried to explain that we were just passing through town, and joining the parade was the only way for us to do it. He just laughed and held out the tickets—one for each of us. I tried not to take them. But he shoved them in my face, and I took them anyway and drove on through town, waving and smiling to the crowd.

It wasn't until we were well on our way again on the other side of town when I heard Mother laughing to herself. "Read your free ticket," she said. When I finally did, this is what I read. **"This is a free ticket. It's good for nothing, but it's free."** What fun we had over that. It helped make our long trip much more enjoyable. I still have that ticket.

Our driving through town with the parade did not happen on a Sabbath as did Ellen's delay on her trip west. But I felt something in common with her about it. We had had a delightful interruption on our trip west, and we enjoyed it. These, I believe, are some of life's extras and should be enjoyed to the full.

I have added this happy little episode, to remind myself and others, Enjoy whatever comes your way, even the surprises. They can be fun. Sabbath can be like this, too, and maybe the unexpected is just one of God's small extras that make Sabbath so enjoyable. After all, He created it as a day for us to stop a while and spend it especially with Him. He loves all of us that much.

1. Ellen G. White Estate, "Spirit of Prophecy Emphasis Week for Seventh-day Adventist Schools, 1968," 43.

2. Ibid.

3. Ellen G. White Estate, "Spirit of Prophecy Emphasis Week for Seventh-day Adventist Schools, 1969," 7.

4. "Spirit of Prophecy Emphasis Week, 1968," 42, 43.

5. *Review and Herald,* February 10, 1885.

6. *Review and Herald,* October 18, 1898.

7. "Spirit of Prophecy Emphasis Week, 1968," 41.

8. Ellen G. White Estate, "Spirit of Prophecy Emphasis Week for Seventh-day Adventist Schools, 1972," 53.

CHAPTER EIGHT

Ellen Was a Dynamo

E ven when Ellen White was an elderly woman, her schedule was still crowded with writing, traveling, and speaking. Fortunately, she was able to enjoy other activities, as well. Let's see how she filled her time during those later years, when other people would feel justified in stopping or taking it easy.

The year 1902 found Ellen in her seventies and living at Elmshaven, her home in the Napa Valley of northern California. It's Sunday morning. Ellen, her farm manager, two of his children, and Sara McEnterfer, Ellen White's companion, went for a ride. They rode in a farm wagon that went bumping along a rough mountain road. It didn't stop until they reached their destination, which was seven miles up Howell Mountain. And why were they taking that long, bumpy ride? They were on their way to pick cherries, "small black ones," Ellen said, "which were given to us for the picking."

I remember when I owned several cherry trees, I found the best fruit was always on top. Evidently Ellen felt the same way.

Picture this now. Here was Ellen White, in her seventies, wearing a long dress as was the custom in her day. And what was she doing? Was she sitting in the wagon telling people where to pick the best cherries? No, not only was she on top of that farm wagon, she was reaching up and picking cherries while standing on one of the seats. "I picked eight quarts," she said. Then she added, "We took home a large box of the fruit." And I can almost see her smiling as she added, "So you see, Sister White is not decrepit yet!"[1]

Ellen loved to garden, and she was proud of the things that grew on her land, as we learn from a letter she wrote in 1902. "Our little patch of strawberries bore wonderfully—something as the corn bore last summer. The fruit was of an excellent flavor and very large, some of the berries measuring three and a half inches around, and one four inches. . . . We are using the early apples now. For several weeks we have had applesauce on the table. Our family think much of this dish. We now have all the peaches that we can eat. The grapevines are loaded. The prune trees are bearing so heavily that some of the branches are breaking."[2]

Prune trees—I know what she meant about them. I had an orchard filled with prune trees when I lived in Nampa, Idaho. They were volunteer trees that had originated from a neighbor's place. He said I was wasting my time trying to get them to produce. "They won't even grow," he said. But he had to eat his words a few years later when he saw the fine crops from my prune trees.

During the time Ellen White was living in California, she had an unforgettable experience with a bumper crop of peaches. The incident comes to us from Alma McKibben, who related it in a series of talks she gave in Mountain View, California.

The story goes like this.

It was summer, and camp meeting time was about to begin. Ellen White was scheduled to be the main Sabbath speaker. The weather was extremely hot, and the peaches in Ellen's orchard were almost ripe and would be ready to pick in a day or two. But Ellen's employees wanted to go to camp meeting. They had been working hard, and the thought of a few days off was like a real vacation for them. Yes, they would go to camp meeting.

But the cook in the house, who had really wanted to attend camp meeting, said she would stay in Healdsburg. She just could not see the entire peach crop go to waste. So she volunteered to remain behind and pick the peaches when they were ripe. Sara would not hear of this. She told the cook that she had worked so hard in the kitchen all year that she was entitled to time off and a vacation. Sara said she would stay behind and take care of the peaches so the cook could go to the camp. Nothing would change her mind. She would stay.

Then, just as it was time to start for camp, the weather suddenly turned cool. It was so cool, in fact, that everyone decided to go to camp meeting—even Sara. The peaches, they felt, would not ripen until they came back. So they all left.

Then during the week of camp meeting, one of Ellen's neighbors sent Ellen a message, reporting that the weather had turned hot again, and the peaches had ripened. Some had already fallen. When the cook heard this, she started to pack. "I'll go home," she said, "pick the crop and get it canned before we lose it all."

Sara said, "No." She would take care of the peach crop. She insisted that the cook should stay, enjoy camp meeting, and not worry.

Sara worked hard in the hot weather. But she got the crop picked in time. Next, she sweated over the hot stove, canning the peaches.

She even stayed up one entire night to finish the job. And when it was finished, she carried the jars of fruit down into the basement and placed them in a fruit cellar.

Oh how nice they looked. Row after row of sparkling clear jars of peaches sat on the shelves. Sara was so proud. The job was finally finished and she was exhausted. *Wait until the others get home,* she thought, *they will be so pleased.* She went to her room that night and happily fell asleep as soon as her head touched the pillow.

And the others did see what Sara had done. When they returned home, Sara herded them all into the basement and showed off her handiwork. They praised her for a job well done.

Sometime later, someone heard an explosion, followed by another, and still another. The entire household woke up. The noise came from the basement. Down the stairs they went. Someone opened the door to the fruit cellar, then shut it fast. Glass and peaches were everywhere.

When it was finally quiet again, someone cautiously opened the door, revealing a mess of fruit and glass. It was on the walls, the shelves, the floor, and even on the ceiling. And the jars of peaches that had not broken were oozing with foul-smelling fruit.

Sara was marched upstairs and made to sit in a chair as they gathered around her. What had she done? The entire crop had been destroyed. They made her relate, step by step, how she had processed the peaches.

During the investigation the cook left the room. And when she returned, she carried a small box in her hand. "Did you use any of these?" she asked Sara, holding up a round rubber ring.

Sara looked puzzled and asked, "What's that?" She had been unaware that she needed to place one of those rings between the mouth of the jar and the lid in order to seal it.

Sara was devastated. All the peaches she had canned were spoiled. Worse than that, she was sure Ellen had heard the explosions and the uproar in the kitchen afterward and would want an explanation. What would she say? Sara stood up, pulled herself to her full height, and said, "I'll tell her myself." She slowly went up the stairs, wondering what Ellen White would say.

Ellen listened quietly to Sara's explanation. After Sara had finished, Ellen simply commented, "Experience is a hard teacher, but we never forget her lessons." And that is all Ellen ever said about the spoiled peach crop.

This tells us a lot about the little lady.

No, Ellen White didn't just sit around and write. She found time from her writing to enjoy nature and her gardens. She had help, of course, but who wouldn't at her age?

But think of it, Ellen in her middle seventies, still writing, still traveling, and still speaking. "In 1902 her letters bore postmarks from New York, New Jersey, Tennessee, and many other states. In 1904 and 1905 she visited Washington, D. C.; in 1909, again in the nation's capital, she attended what was to be her last General Conference session. At the first Sabbath meeting she spoke for 50 minutes to a large congregation. Her clear voice could be heard by all under and around the packed tent. The conference lasted through three Sabbaths and Mrs. White preached the morning sermons on the other two Sabbaths also."[3] But what was going on in Elmshaven while Ellen was traveling around the country?

Sara tells us. She said, "There are eight of us engaged in work for Sister White. . . . Some work on her books, some on the articles that are published in the papers, some attend to correspondence, and others are copyists. Most of these workers have been with her for a number of years; some 25 years, some 20, and so on down." She continues, "It falls to my lot to keep track of her correspondence. Sister White always reads every copy after it is prepared by any one of her workers. . . .We as her helpers carry out her wishes to the letter."[4] Her son Willie worked in an office building behind Elmshaven. On a day he must have felt a bit overwhelmed, he described the pace this way: "What are we doing in the office? It is hard to tell. We seem to be like squirrels in a whirligig. We run as fast as we can and keep in the same place all the time, some big things just before and some little things occupying all of our time."[5]

Ellen was a dynamo. There was just no stopping her, even in her seventies. The Lord had given her messages and insights for the Church, some messages of rebuke but more messages of encouragement and hope. Unfortunately, not all readers are able to find the proper balance between the rebuke and the encouragement.

A number of years ago my parents and I were driving across the United States. We didn't want to travel on Sabbath, but on that trip found it necessary to do so. To avoid eating in a restaurant on Sabbath, Mother made a lunch to take with us. My father was not a Seventh-day Adventist, but he went along with the plan.

We were in the middle of one of the western states, and it was Sabbath. There was nothing but sagebrush and sand for miles. About noon we saw a sign stating a rest area was ahead. We pulled in and found trees, green grass, and tables. It was like an oasis to us. I noticed other people stopping also.

Oh, that lunch tasted good. After eating we relaxed before continuing on. It was then that I noticed something quite unusual. Three teenagers, two boys and one girl, were sitting at tables and reading books. That wasn't what was so unusual. The strange thing was that all of those teenagers were sitting at separate tables, and there was a wide distance between them.

Since I worked for a publisher I was curious as to what they were reading. There was no communication between the three, and they were deeply engrossed in their books. Had I stumbled across a secret that my publisher should know about? What were those books? I had to know.

I walked over to where the girl was reading and sat down across from her. She didn't look up. I asked her what she was reading. Without taking her eyes from the page she held up the book. I was shocked. It was a book by Ellen White.

I couldn't believe what I was seeing. I said, "I work for the publisher who prints those books. I work for the Pacific Press." Then I followed this with a question. "Are you a Seventh-day Adventist?"

The girl's answer made my temper rise. "Yes," she answered. "My parents are in that trailer over there, and they are watching us. My brothers and I are supposed to read these books. And we are not to talk to anyone or to each other. And when we have finished, we will have a test on what we read." The girl wouldn't say any more as she kept on reading, but I noticed a trace of fear in her eyes.

When I returned to my parents, I let loose my pent-up anger. "I am going over to that trailer and tell off those so-called Seventh-day Adventists. They are destroying their children for the church."

I started for the trailer, but Mother called me back. "Don't," she said. "It will only cause trouble."

So out of respect for Mother's wishes, I returned to our table.

We drove away soon after that. And as we did, I looked back and saw three children, at separate tables, reading books they did not want to read—the writings of Ellen G. White.

I have thought of this encounter many times since. And I am almost certain that the three children I saw that day no longer read the books of Ellen White or even attend a church, any church. Force destroys. Those three teenagers were learning to dislike church, Ellen White, and all things religious because their parents were misusing the writings of Ellen White. Those teenagers would probably miss out on the hope and encouragement that a proper study of Ellen's writing could provide.

---

1. Ellen G. White Estate, "Spirit of Prophecy Emphasis Week for Seventh-day Adventist Schools, 1972," 56.
2. Ibid.
3. Ibid., 57, 58.
4. Ibid., 56.
5. Ibid., 57.

CHAPTER NINE

She Said
It Was OK

Let's turn for a moment now to one of Ellen's children, a boy named William, Willie for short. We can get a glimpse of Ellen and James White as parents and Ellen as a grandmother through their interaction with Willie over the years.

Willie, Ellen and James White's youngest child, was as normal as any boy could be. And, like other children, he didn't always obey. One Sabbath the Whites had guests from out of town. They spent the morning at church and then attended an exceptionally long afternoon meeting. Willie was bored.

After sundown when supper was over, he was put to bed and told to stay there. I take it that because he was told to stay there, we can assume that he didn't always stay in bed once he got there. And I believe I am right.

Willie stayed in bed all right, but he couldn't go to sleep. He listened, instead, to what was being said in the other room. Suddenly he sat straight up when he heard someone say, "Let's sing." Willie loved to sing.

In a few minutes Edson, his older brother, began to play on their pump organ. Everybody sang, including Willie. He sang as loudly as he could from his bed. The Whites' visitors began to laugh. They thought it was cute. Then quite suddenly, and now in Willie's own words, we read what happened next. "I jumped out of bed, and in my nightgown, marched out into the large room among the visitors. Father picked me up and put me back to bed."

But that was not the end of the story. "Again the company sang and I joined my voice with theirs, and soon reappeared among them. And again Father put me back to bed, with strict orders to stay there."

Did he stay there? Willie has more to tell us. "But I had by this time become excited. . . . I got up the third time and marched out among the company of singers. Then Father picked me up and took me out through the kitchen, to the back porch. There he laid me across his knee and administered a hearty spanking."

Did it work?

"This," he said, "enabled me to see clearly where I had erred." He continues, "I remember today how everything looked, especially the position of the moon as it hung over the boys' workshop. I thought seriously of my evil deeds, and resolved to be good."

I'd say that Willie learned how to sing a new song that night.

Willie finished this story by saying that this was the only time his father spanked him.[1]

Now that Willie had learned his lesson, was he good from then on? Ellen reminded him of another time he was disciplined. Willie claimed he didn't remember. Again, we have the account in Willie's own words.

"[Mother] was reading while holding me on her lap. I raised my head in such a way as to interfere with her reading. She gently pushed it down. I resisted and persisted and she continued to put my head out of the way. Then I became angry and manifested rebellion. In response to this she spanked me vigorously.

"Mother's government," he continued, "though firm, was yet so kind that her boys had no heart to resist it."[2]

"Ellen White was most concerned that children be taught to make their own decisions and that their decisions should be right ones. She did not believe in 'iron rule' which leads to a lack of self-confidence. But she did believe children need to be guided by consecrated parents and teachers. 'There is danger of both parents and teachers commanding and dictating too much, while they fail to come sufficiently into social relation with their children or scholars,' she wrote. In simpler language she was saying, 'Be friends with your children, at home or in school.' 'Manifest an interest in all their efforts and even in their sports.' And as for teachers, she wrote that it is more important for a teacher to be a real Christian than for him to hold many graduate degrees."[3]

Let's go way back to a time when Willie was far too young to be bad or disobey. He was just a baby. Willie told this story long after his mother had died.

In the early 1850s James White's sister Anna came to live with the Whites. She had tuberculosis and was not expected to live long. She instantly fell in love with baby Willie. Not realizing she could transfer the dreaded disease to her baby nephew, she began to play with him. She would pick him up and carry him around, hugging and kissing him. Ellen was beside herself with fear because she knew Willie could become ill. So whenever Anna picked Willie up, Ellen tried to think of some excuse for taking the baby from her. It didn't work. Anna just held him closer, all the time breathing in his face.

Ellen decided that to protect her baby and not hurt her sister-in-law's feelings, she had to do something desperate. It was something she did not want to do, but she felt she had to. Whenever she

saw Anna pick Willie up to play with him, Ellen came over beside
them. And without Anna's realizing it, Ellen would slyly reach up
under baby Willie's clothes and pinch him. She didn't do it gently—she bore down hard.

Of course Willie's face turned red as he opened his mouth
and screamed. He would kick and squirm so wildly that Anna
quickly handed the baby to Ellen saying, "Take him, I can't handle
him!"

Ellen would hurry screaming Willie into another room, where
she quieted him down and gently rubbed the spot where she had
pinched. Her plan worked every time. And as the days went by
Anna paid less and less attention to the baby.

Ellen had solved a delicate situation by not hurting Anna's
feelings and at the same time protecting her child during the short
time Anna had left to live.[4]

What was Sabbath like in the Whites' home when their children were growing up? "The Whites had a regular daily program.
Even on Sabbath the boys were up early. Chickens, horses and
cows were all cared for before worship. After breakfast Henry,
Edson and Willie, wearing their Sabbath clothes, walked to church,
followed by their parents. Often they heard their father preach,
then sometimes their mother as she 'exhorted' [advised or cau-
tioned] the congregation; sometimes she told of a vision God had
given her. Their Sabbath afternoons were spent reading, walking
in the woods or out to Goguac Lake or down by the river. Sometimes they made missionary visits. Sabbath was the best day of
the week. For sundown worship Henry played the old-fashioned
organ and the others sang with a fervor that echoed far down the
street."[5]

After James White died, Willie took over the job of looking
after his mother. And he was doing a good job. The following
story gives us an example of how good.

He and Ellen were in New Zealand. It was camp meeting time, and Ellen was not well. However, as she so often did, she woke up early and began writing at about 3:00 A.M. Around 5:00 she decided she was well enough to go to the 5:30 meeting at the campground, which was only about a mile away from where she was staying.

Thinking no one else was awake, Ellen quietly left the house and went into the barn. Once there, she found what she was looking for—a two-wheeled cart. The horse was in its stall and ready to go. It was Ellen's plan to harness the horse to the cart and drive to the campground. But now she had a problem. The harness was too high on the wall for her to reach. *I'll walk,* she told herself. *It isn't far, and I'm feeling better.*

So off she started for the campground.

Ellen made slow progress because she stopped every few minutes to rest and catch her breath. She was still quite weak from being sick, but she kept going.

Suddenly she heard a noise behind her. Turning around, she saw something coming toward her. It looked like a cart. Then she thought her eyes were playing tricks on her in the early morning mist. There was no horse pulling the cart, yet it was coming closer and closer.

When she realized what was going on, a smile spread across her face. Then she laughed. Because what she saw was the two-wheeled cart she had seen in the barn, and Willie was pulling it. He was huffing and puffing as he ran with the cart behind him.

A noise outside the house had wakened him. And when he looked out a window, he saw his mother walking down the road toward the campground. He leaped into his clothes and ran for the barn. There was no time to harness the horse, so he grabbed the shafts and started running, pulling the cart behind him.

"Mother!" he shouted. "Wait!"

She waited.

He stopped beside her but by then couldn't talk because he was out of breath. He just motioned for her to get in the seat. Finally he managed to say, "You shouldn't be out here like this! Please get in!"

"Willie," she laughed, "whatever are you doing? You shouldn't be out here like this either! I'm too heavy for you to pull by yourself. And what will people think when they see you acting like a horse?"

Now it was Willie's turn to laugh. "They will think that I'm just an old work horse. Now, let's get going so we won't be late to the meeting."

And off they went, with Ellen White laughing to herself.

Someone spotted them as they came near the campground. And Elder Starr came running to help Willie. Together the two of them pulled that cart up to the entrance of the main tent. People who saw them smiled and laughed. They had never seen horses like that before.

Willie didn't stay for the meeting. He went back to the house, finished dressing, then returned for his mother with a real horse pulling the cart.[6]

At another time Ellen recalled something about Willie that made her laugh outright. She was giving a sermon when she noticed smiles in the audience. Not only that, some of those smiles turned into muffled laughs. She wondered what was going on. She hadn't said anything to make them laugh. Seeing that most of the audience was looking past her, she turned around.

And there, sitting among the line of ministers was Willie, and he was fast asleep. She interrupted her sermon, leaned over the pulpit, and spoke softly to the congregation. "When Willie was a baby," she said, "James and I traveled a great deal. We used to put him to sleep in a little basket right in front of the pulpit where we could watch him. There he slept peacefully during all our sermons." She paused then added, "Apparently he has not gotten out of the habit."[7]

Francis White, one of Willie's children, worked at the Pacific Press. We became good friends. I asked him once if he had known his grandmother.

"No," he answered. "I was too young, but I was told that I sat on her lap sometimes and played with the buttons on her dress."

"Tell me about you father, Willie," I requested.

"He was the best father in the world," he answered. "He used to be gone a lot on long trips. And when he came home, he was often wearing a long black overcoat. He would walk into the house with his hands up in the air. This was a signal for us children. We would run to him, and with his hands and arms still held high, we would go through his pockets. We were never disappointed, because we would find small gifts there for each one of us."

I never found time to ask Frankie, as we called him, about his father again, and I have often regretted that.

Ellen loved children. "She usually had in her home from one to six boys and girls whom she was mothering. When she heard of a sick, discouraged, or unfortunate person, the one question was whether there might be room at the table for another plate, or a corner somewhere in the house for an extra cot."[7]

A number of years ago, while on a research trip to the White Estate, I happened to find a small pamphlet that took my attention. The author told about the time when she, as a child, was living in Ellen's home. She wrote that other children were living there too. They were not Ellen's own children, but Ellen treated them as if they were. They played games, colored pictures, listened to stories, and took walks together. They even cut pictures from magazines and pasted them in scrapbooks. The scissors, she noted, never had pointed blades; they were round tipped and blunt so that the children could not cut themselves. Worship time was special, with each child taking part—something the author never forgot. Children who lived in the house, and even those who came to visit, called Ellen White "Mother." She loved boys and girls; they knew it and loved her back.

But there was some special, unexpected information in that little pamphlet that made me smile. It told me that Ellen White knew more about children and what made them happy than we thought she did. I won't tell yet what made me smile; I'll save that for later. Just keep reading—and you will soon know what it was.

I had been asked to speak to a group of junior-aged boys and girls at Pinecrest youth camp in the Sierras. My main assignment was to tell stories about Ellen White to these Seventh-day Adventist children. For a change, everyone was listening quietly as I told story after story. This was unusual during an outing at a summer camp. I knew the children were filled with energy.

Suddenly I realized that I was telling a story I had not planned to tell. And as I got into it, I knew I had made a mistake. *The children should not hear this,* I thought to myself. But I couldn't back out of telling the story once I started. Worst of all, the children were listening to every word I said. I had to continue. And I did.

I knew instinctively there would be a reaction to the story. And sure enough, there was. On Saturday night we heard yells and screams. Children were leaping on and off beds. They shouted as they chased each other. Some were even rolling on the floor. But they were all laughing. They were having the time of their lives and loving every second of it.

I glanced at the counselors. They shrugged their shoulders, rolled their eyes, threw their hands in the air, and said it was all my fault.

What was going on? Those children were having a grand knock-down, blow-after-blow pillow fight. And the reason no one could stop it was a fact the woman had included in that pamphlet. She said that once in a while, Ellen White allowed the children in her home to have pillow fights. She didn't allow pillow fights often, but when she did, the children went at it with all the energy their little bodies could produce.

What a time those children had at Pinecrest summer camp. No one got hurt. And happy to say, they all slept well that night. They had used up all their pent-up energy and wore themselves out. But most of all, while they were having that grand pillow fight, no one could stop it. They couldn't, because Ellen White said it was OK.

We have seen how Ellen mothered not just her sons, but other children who needed a home as well. Now let's turn our attention to Willie's own children and watch how Ellen enjoyed being a grandmother. Herbert and Henry were twins. She had lost two of her own sons in death—Henry, her oldest, and Herbert, her youngest. Ellen must have been delighted when the twins were named after their uncles.

A few diary pages, along with a letter or two, tell us how much she loved Willie's twin boys. Most of the entries are from Australia, where most of the roads in the bush country were muddy, rough, or dusty. But the bumpier they were, the more the boys liked them.

"The boys are hearty fellows," she wrote Willie in 1897, who was in the United States at the time. "I think it will cost you something to feed them. They can take a few steps now, and are in good health. Today Herbert put his finger in Henry's mouth, and Henry bit it. Oh, how Herbert did cry! For some time he would not look at Henry without crying."

"Wednesday, June 30, 1897. We rode to the post office. The twins, Herbert and James Henry, saw the horse and wagon at the door and both came running to their grandmother with their little arms outstretched, full of expectation that I would take them [to the post office]. I did not have the heart to disappoint them. Their wraps were thrown on and Sara cared for one and I the other, and then they were perfectly happy, having a hold of the end of the lines [of the horse] and supposing that they were driving."

"Tuesday, May 10, 1898. Sara and I rode out about two miles to a lemon orchard. . . . We obtained the native lemons for twopence a dozen—four cents in American money. . . . The twins . . . now 25 months old, were very much pleased gathering the lemons and piling them up in heaps, and with their unintelligible language showing them to grandma."

"Friday, May 20, 1898. The twins . . . are very interesting little fellows, chattering to the birds and to the logging bullock teams which we met."

"Monday, June 27, 1898. Sara and I backed our platform wagon under the trees and then Sara could stand up in the wagon and pick the lemons. The two-year-and-half twins enjoyed this very much, but their hands were not strong enough to pull the lemons from their firm fastening. Sara pulled fruit for them. These are dear little fellows."

"Sunday, September 4, 1898. Willie, May [his wife] and the children—Mabel [Willie's daughter], and the twins—went with me to the workers' railroad builders' camp. I spoke to about one dozen women. The men kept afar off."[8]

There are two entries now from Willie himself. They tell something about his entire family. They were a hard-working bunch.

"Ella [another daughter] takes care of the cow, and sometimes has long tramps to find her. You would laugh to see her some rainy mornings with her big rubber boots, splashing through the mud, and driving her cows to pasture. Mabel . . . loves to attend the babies and split kindling wood. In fact she loves to chop, and is quite expert with the axe."

"I take care of the horse, May looks after the chickens, and Mabel feeds the cats. Henry and Herbert put in most of their time feeding themselves. They are growing finely, and begin to respond when you talk with them. Their vocabulary is not large, but they can say goo and gee and gaa, and when they are hungry they can yell loud enough to be heard to the police station."[9]

Ellen's family sounds like a normal family to me. Their stories reveal Ellen White as a firm but loving mother giving spankings but allowing pillow fights and as a doting grandmother taking twin grandsons with her to the post office and to a lemon orchard.

1. Ellen G. White Estate, "Spirit of Prophecy Emphasis Week for Seventh-day Adventist Schools, 1972," 26, 27.
2. Ibid.
3. Ibid., 7.
4. Ibid., 21.
5. Ibid., 23.
6. Ellen G. White Estate, "The Spirit of Prophecy Emphasis Week for Seventh-day Adventist Schools, 1985," 26, 27.
7. Ellen G. White Estate, "The Spirit of Prophecy Emphasis Week for Seventh-day Adventist Schools, 1972," 50.
8. Ibid., 46-48.
9. Ibid., 46-50.

If you enjoyed this book, you'll enjoy these as well:

Ellen White: Friend of Angels
Paul B. Ricchiuti. Seeks to show us who Ellen White was, instead of concentrating on what she did. As he draws from little known stories about her life, the personality and character of the prophet, wife, and mother emerges in this warm account of a truly amazing woman.
0-8163-1707-0. Paperback.
US$8.99, Can$14.49.

His Messenger
Ruth Wheeler. A classic biography on the life and work of Ellen White written originally for young people.
0-8163-1885-9. US$9.99, Can$15.99.